JAPANESE RAGE

JAPANESE
BUSINESS
AND ITS
ASSAULT ON
THE WEST

JAPANESE RAGE

LEON ANDERSON

FOUR WALLS EIGHT WINDOWS, NEW YORK

Published by:
Four Walls Eight Windows
PO Box 548, Village Station
New York, NY 10014

First Edition
First Printing April 1992

Library of Congress Cataloging-in-Publication Data:
Anderson, Leon, 1937-
Japanese Rage: Japanese Business and its Assault on the West
by Leon Anderson.—1st ed.
p. cm.
ISBM: 0-941423-59-X (cloth)
1. Japan—Foreign economic relations—United States.
2. United States—Foreign economic relations—Japan.
3. National characteristics, Japanese.
4. Morita, Akio, 1921- "No" to ieru Nihon.
I. Title.
HF1602.15U6A46 1991
337.52073—dc20   90-25372
CIP

Book design by Cindy LaBreacht
Printed in the U.S.A.

This book is for

Barbara L. Anderson, my wife of 31 years, and for

Inez R. Anderson-Coleman, my mother.

The crane stops and stares

The crab passes unawares

One eats, the other dies

TABLE OF CONTENTS

ACKNOWLEDGEMENTS

The research assistance of Eva S. Csige, an economics graduate student in the Drexel University doctoral program, is greatly appreciated. The staff at the New York Metropolitan Library, the Princeton University Library and the New Jersey State Library at Trenton are all to be thanked for their professional assistance. I also want to thank my wife, Barbara, for her moral support and her assistance in researching this book, my son Michael and his wife Pamela, and my son, Paul, for their support during this otherwise difficult time in our lives. They were wonderful.

PREFACE

When I decided to write this book my goal was to be brief, to get to the point quickly and be done with it. I hate jargon. More than that, I despise obfuscation and people who muddy the waters so that you can't see through to the grit lying on the bottom. Unfortunately, there has been so much muck stirred up on the subject of Japan that the waters may never again come clean. Partly, this is the result of the Japanese themselves interfering in Western academic research. They see it as promoting Japanese-American relations.

However, the fact is that the largest and most available sources of funding for research on Japan-related issues are found in Japan. Professors from respected universities have been lured by this Japanese money and have accepted it because it was the most readily available source of funds for their projects. The problem with this arrangement is that their work becomes suspect. If they want to get funding for the next year, or the next phase of their project, the conclusions they draw in the early stages need to cast Japan in a favorable light. You need only look at the official translation of Akio Morita and Shintaro Ishihara's book, *The Japan That Can Say No*, for confirmation of this fact.

This is not a textbook. The subject is far too important to be relegated to academia or to get bogged down in minutiae. It is my sincere hope that people without any special education will be able to pick up this book and understand everything, easily.

In Desmond Morris's introduction to his wonderful book on the evolution of man, *The Naked Ape*, Morris, no professional anthropologist or archaeologist, explains how important it was for some person to rise above the various, and often competing, branches of science and draw together the loose strands of information.

This is a role to which I aspire. There is so much information floating around on Japan that it is overwhelming. Most authors tend to take one facet of Japan and write at great length about that subject. I have tried to examine the whole scene in order to provide the reader with reasons for why the Japanese behave as they do.

Like many, I was incensed when I read an unauthorized English translation of Akio Morita and Shintaro Ishihara's book, *The Japan That Can Say No*. Its tone was arrogant and it denigrated America. When the long-delayed official translation was finally released, it was limited to Ishihara's sections only. This was easy enough to do because they each wrote separate chapters and Morita just deleted his. Akio Morita, the Chairman of the Board of Sony Corporation, kept his name off the English version for fear that Sony's business might be hurt. The official version was translated by a Japan-apologist professor from Harvard University who managed to take the hard, threatening edge off most of Ishihara's comments about the United States, and to settle on a tone of benign rebuke. I have discussed many of Morita's and Ishihara's points in this book, comparing both translations where possible. It's also important to understand that some of the departments and agencies of the U.S. government are regularly selling out the nation so that they can advance their own private interests.

In this same vein it becomes important to ask why Ronald Reagan went to Japan and accepted two million dollars soon after leaving the White House. Supposedly, the money was an honorarium for making a speech. It looks more like a pay-off for selling out his country to the Japanese during his administration. Greed will loom large as a subject in this book.

This is not a Japan-bashing book. On the contrary, my feelings about the Japanese are split down the middle. I admire the Japanese, but am wary of them. I cannot help respecting their business acumen and drive, but their materialism is unrestrained, and is causing the Western world some real problems.

There are ultra-conservative influences in Japan's ruling Liberal Democratic Party that are downright dangerous to world peace. Americans should know about them, and plan now on how to deal with them. I have tried to throw some light on these areas and to expose the direction of their expanding influence amongst client states and world politicians. Often, the real power in Japan is not even in the government; it frequently stands outside of the public sphere.

My business is consulting on international trade opportunities, and I have done a lot of work in product development. My company, Anderson Direct Response, Inc. began in 1982 with a concentration in the area of direct response (mail order) marketing, both domestic and international. I have traveled throughout Japan and dealt with Japanese companies, large and small, for many years. Japan has been a subject of my research and pleasure reading for most of my adult life.

LEON ANDERSON
March 1992

CHAPTER ONE
Perspectives

In 1989 a formidable and frightening book was published in Japan. It was called *The Japan That Can Say No*, and it was rabidly anti-American. The book outlined Japan's major complaints against the United States and its Western European trading partners. The authors are Akio Morita, Chairman of the Board of the Sony Corporation, and Shintaro Ishihara, a writer turned politician and one-time rising star in Japan's Liberal Democratic Party. Ishihara had been the Minister of Transport under Prime Minister Noboru Takeshita (1987-1989), and ran for president of the Liberal Democratic Party (L.D.P.) in August 1989. He also seems to have had a significant voice in trade policy. This influence is probably due to his wide popular support and to his being a core member of the party's ultra-conservative wing.

After a series of critical articles in the Western press, an expurgated, less vitriolic, version of *The Japan That Can Say No* (Simon & Schuster) was released in the United States in January 1991 under Ishihara's name only. Morita didn't want anything to do with this edition, and tried to distance himself from the book. Some additional pages by Ishihara were included, in which he equivocated his position and offered some hope for future American trade opportunities in Japan.

In the summer of 1990, Ishihara published a second book, available in Japanese only, titled *Still The Japan That Can Say No*. It offered nothing new. It simply reinforced what had

1

been said in his first book. However, the book became an immediate bestseller in Japan, which indicates that his Japan-first message is not falling on deaf ears at home. Morita did not participate in this follow-up version of *The Japan That Can Say No*. In fact, he seems to be somewhat surprised and embarrassed by the negative reception accorded his first book in the United States. He refused my request to interview him on the subject, and instead relies on Sony's public relations manager to spill oil on these troubled waters. Having criticized the United States in print, Morita now seems to want the whole episode to just go away lest Sony's business be hurt. Perhaps someday he will clarify his position.

In the meantime, the whole question of Japanese attitudes toward the United States and its Western European trading partners is still open to interpretation. To anyone who has followed the course of Japanese-American trade and political relations in this century, the truth behind many Japanese attitudes is evident. Older American citizens who were reading the newspapers sixty years ago in the 1930s must be struck by the similarity of the issues relating to trade and politics now confronting Japan and America in the 1990s. These issues also confront the United Kingdom, whose influence in Hong Kong, Singapore, India, Australia and New Zealand, is quickly being supplanted by Japan's economic might.

The most significant difference between Japanese-American relations then and now lies in the changing nature of trading patterns. In 1931, Japan and the United States were complementary trading partners. That is, the Western world bought Japanese raw silk and cheap, labor-intensive toys, dolls, garments and canned foods. In return, the United States shipped cotton, automobiles, machine tools, oil and petroleum products, chemicals and scrap iron. Each country received exactly what it needed without serious disruption of the other's domestic industrial structure.

In fact, the United States was then, and is today, the single most important customer of Japan. In 1931, the United States bought 40 percent of all Japanese exports.[1] Raw silk alone accounted for about 70 percent of the American purchases. This was extremely favorable trade, the best kind available. It is the kind of trade that economics professors refer to when they write philosophically about the ideal structure of world trade. Each country exports its best products, and neither disrupts the other's markets or industrial base by introducing products generated with the aid of artificial support mechanisms, e.g., government subsidies, discriminatory tariffs or unreasonably regulated home markets.

However, as beneficial as trade was between East and West in 1931, it was occasionally marked by dispute. There was, for example, a small, but vocal, protectionist sentiment growing in the United States, especially in the toy and garment industries. This movement was only to be expected as the toy and garment industries were the very ones where Japanese and American business talents came most into conflict. It was in these areas, however small, where Japanese-American trade was competitive rather than complementary. They were also labor-intensive industries, where even depression-level American wages were much higher than Japanese wages. But because the conflict was small it was ignored. The United States continued to ignore it, and continued to avoid making the machine tool investments that were necessary to improve labor productivity, until the 1990s arrived, and with it the prospect of Japanese ownership of America.

In the 1990s, the nature of Japanese trade with the rest of the world has changed dramatically. Instead of essentially complementary trade, the Japanese are now competing with almost every industry in the Western world. Instead of concentrating on labor-intensive products, as one might expect from 123 million people crowded onto a few small islands, the Japanese have developed a trade strategy designed to propel their nation into world economic dominance. The danger of this policy is that if Japan is allowed to succeed further, their export customers will begin to collapse economically. Beginning with the United States, which in 1990 still took 35 percent of Japan's total exports, the West will find itself increasingly unable to finance further purchases.[2] For this reason, America feels a desperate need to rewrite the trade rules between itself and Japan.

The essential similarity between Japanese-American relations in the 1930s and the 1990s is the tension between the two countries over Japan's aggressive trade policy. Even in the officially translated version of his book, Ishihara's words are harsh and to the point, "The industrialized capitalist countries are engaged in severe economic competition, if not a trade war."[3] Following the Manchurian Incident in 1931, in which Japanese soldiers provoked a confrontation with the Manchurian militia that resulted in thousands of Chinese casualties and the capture of the province, the United States criticized Japan's militaristic methods of expanding their trade opportunities, and began to impose some increasingly severe trade sanctions against Japan.

In the 1990s, the Japanese are no less dedicated to securing their Asian markets and world trade position than they were sixty years ago. The difference is that they have found a better way to accomplish their goal. Imperialism based on the sword proved to be a terribly costly policy. However, economic imperialism works just as well, and the Japanese have become masters of economic warfare. The goal of either kind of warfare is dominance and control of markets.

The Japanese well understand that the power which controls the economy also controls the political arena. This is why they have made such an effort to befriend the office of the United States Trade Representative (U.S.T.R.). The major United States trade policy organization, the U.S.T.R., is dominated by lawyers rather than economists or salespeople from corporate America. It has been easy for the Japanese to convince these democratically minded representatives that they should not be too hard on Japan's modest efforts to expand their trade. Lawyers are suckers for equal-opportunity arguments, especially lawyers whose incomes have derived from Japanese clients, and whose incomes in the future will likely come from the same source. Economists or salespeople, on the other hand, understand what it takes to keep a factory going, and what it means to compete for orders in a price conscious market against a competitor who operates from a protected home base.

Far too many negotiators in the U.S.T.R., from the top down, are heavily associated with Japanese industry. Chapter Twelve, "Spies—The United States Trade Representative's Office," explores this problem in greater detail. And, far too much of their family income is derived from Japanese sources. Some of these U.S.T.R. employees are married to native Japanese spouses, or were themselves educated in Japan. Some have had businesses in Japan or have relatives with businesses in Japan. According to a front page article in *The Wall Street Journal* on February 23, 1990, since the early 1970s, 20 of the former top 60 U.S.T.R. officials have gone on to represent foreign clients, many for Japanese companies. At one point in *The Japan That Can Say No*, Ishihara calls the U.S.T.R. representative a spy for Japan.[4] In short, the U.S.T.R. personnel relationships, though currently legal, represent the sort of behavior that would get one prosecuted for felonious conflict of interest in private business.

The second half of the Japanese imperialist dilemma is what to do with all the people on their tiny islands. It's a country a little smaller than the size of California, but with roughly four times the population density. Finding enough habitable land has long been a problem. Real estate prices have reached absurd levels in Japan. Because the country is so mountainous, there hasn't been enough available land for over a hundred years to grow the food necessary to be self-sufficient without enormous subsidies, much less to provide reasonable housing. Emigration in mass numbers was the answer Japan saw in 1931, and is clearly still an open question in Japan today. Japan's need for Siberia or Manchuria is as essential now as it was sixty years ago. This is one reason Japan resents America's political intrusion in Asian affairs, and sees it as a threat to its long-term security.[5]

The United States has been exceedingly generous to its former enemy. When the war ended, the U.S. did not exact reparations for Japanese atrocities. America forgave them for the Bataan Death March and their treatment of allied prisoners. America put Pearl Harbor in the past, and accepted the loss of millions of people in the Pacific War as the cost of failed diplomacy. The United States helped Japan rebuild its cities and economy.

The United States is still Japan's largest single customer for its export products. The United States' balance of payments deficit with Japan has been running between 40 billion dollars and 56 billion dollars per year since 1986 and has been in a major deficit position for over a decade. No other country in the world even comes close to spending 50 billion dollars a year with Japan, much less running that amount as a deficit. South Korea, Taiwan and Germany are Japan's next best trading partners, and they each bought less than 20 billion dollars worth of Japan's exports in 1990.[7] The fact is that the United States has not hindered Japan's economic growth. Rather, it has been the world's most important supporter of Japan's economic expansion.

American consumers have been repaid with allegations of prejudice, and with diplomatic double-talk indistinguishable from Special Envoy Saburo Kurusu's talks with Secretary of State Cordell Hull in December 1941. "We want peace," Saburo told Hull, as the Japanese fleet was sailing to attack Pearl Harbor. Today the Japanese again want peace, but it must be on their terms, with world ports open to their container ships.

Obviously, Morita and Ishihara's message has to be taken seriously. These men occupy important roles in Japanese society, and their decisions have worldwide impact. Actually, their book is a classic "Good Cop, Bad Cop" routine. Morita is the soft voice gently urging and cajoling the United States to open its mouth and take the medicine Ishihara is prescribing.

"It won't hurt," Morita seems to be saying. "You have been on top for so long, it is time to let Japan take over." If he ever left Sony, Morita could easily make a good living as a stage hypnotist. Ishihara waves the katana sword and calls the United States "mad dogs." He thinks it is time to tell the United States "no." He does not believe that Japan should be bound by American rules not to sell semiconductors to the former Soviet States or machine tools to anybody who can pay for them. No, and I paraphrase, Japan should not change its trade policies simply to make it easier for America to invade its Asian markets. No, Japan should not feel bound to a defense armaments structure designed by the United States.

This brings us to another facet of the Japanese character that needs to be understood. In Japan, "inferior" people bow to the wishes of their betters or say whatever is necessary to propitiate them. In the West, this behavior is known as "lying." In Japan, it is what is expected. When the Japanese negotiate they expect their counterparts, Americans or Europeans, to see the wisdom of their proposal, though it has not been expressed in so many words, and to grant them their wishes. This process is called *ishin denshin*, and it means knowing what another person is thinking so that he doesn't have to say it. After all, to many Japanese, Americans are barbarians, and should be made aware of the importance of serving the higher good. It is up to the United States to service their needs, to stand in the vanguard and break the waves. Many Japanese see the United States' role as one of paving the way for the greater glory of the higher civilization: their civilization.

The truth in these circumstances is ephemeral. It may well be all right to agree not to sell certain technology to Iran if in the process Japan wins the license to manufacture the item. But how long does the promise hold? It becomes problematic, but the solution will serve Japan's interests, you can be sure.

The New York Times reported on February 23, 1990, concerning Secretary of Defense Richard Cheney's Asian tour, "Japanese officials say privately that they are worried that an overall reduction of the American (troop) presence in Asia would reawaken fears in other parts of the region about the growing influence of Japan."

It has become doctrine among Japanese defense department officials, including the authors of *The Japan That Can Say No*, that the American troop presence in Asia must be maintained for the immediate future. What is not expressed so openly is that the primary purpose of an American military presence in Asia is to camouflage the growing power and influence of Japan. The United States' role in Asia now is to be a smoke screen for Japan, since it is no longer needed as a protection against the Soviet Union. Not surprisingly, Japan was willing to increase its share of the expense of maintaining U.S. troops in Japan. As a result of

Secretary Cheney's visit, the Japanese now pay for a paltry 40 percent of the expense of maintaining those forces. It is a bargain price to have America provide a decorative *shoji* screen for Japanese expansionist policies.

What follows in this book is an analysis of the Japanese people's attitudes toward the United States and Western Europe. It is an evaluation of their diplomatic demands in the light of historical perspective as well as an attempt to decipher the often unspoken long-range goals of the Japanese government. Most importantly, it is an attempt to reveal the weaknesses in America's government, and how its social and economic structures have contributed to its own ruin.

Morita says it best when he claims that the Japanese think and speak differently than do Westerners. This is true far beyond the usual difficulties that Western nations have in translating each other's languages and cultures. Most Western countries at least share common religions and similar cultural heritages. They have traded with, and waged war against each other for so many centuries that they have come to understand each other fairly well and share many of the same values.

This is not the case with Japan. Culture often interferes with communication. It is difficult to say no in Japan or to speak frankly with a stranger. One reason for Morita and Ishihara's book was to encourage other Japanese to learn how to say no. The Japanese often have a way of assuming that if they wish hard enough for something, their Western clients will eventually understand and grant them their wish. They persist in this belief, even if the spoken, signed and sealed words say something entirely different. Worse, they continue to act on their wishes to the detriment of the signed and sealed words of any treaties that have been negotiated. This was the cause of the blow-up between

Toshiba and the U.S. Congress over the sale of machine tools to the Soviet Union.

The Japanese live their lives around narrowly defined company activities. If you are not part of the company, or worse, if you are not Japanese, then you are not part of their world. To many Japanese, Westerners are barbarians (*gaijin*) beneath contempt. It pays to remember this fact.

Edwin O. Reischauer, former U.S. Ambassador to Japan, described the situation best in his book, *The Japanese*, when he said, "Group associations, by emphasizing discrete hierarchical relationships and reducing lateral contacts with groups of similar function and status, play down class feelings as these are known in the West."[8] In examining the class structure of Japanese society, Reischauer remarks that almost everyone believes that he or she belongs to the middle class. He might have said more accurately that most people define themselves as equal members of a clique.

What the Westerner confronts, then, on visiting Japan, is a closed society of private associations. The Japanese rarely fraternize, even with each other, outside their own rigidly defined company or special activity group, such as a tea ceremony or martial arts school. The Westerner looking for a club where he can be introduced to the "right sorts" of people, will be disappointed. These clubs don't exist. There is almost no way to meet Japanese people outside of a formal business context. They are masters at keeping these occasions polite, but impersonal.

On reading this, a fair-minded Westerner might respond skeptically, thinking that perhaps I am being too critical. Americans' normal reaction to such charges is to be charitable and to make allowances for foreigners. Frankly, this is exactly what Morita, Ishihara and the others in the Ministry of International Trade and Industry are counting on. Ishihara says in one passage of his book, "...the poor Japanese politicians have never studied these issues..." Or, in the official version, "Japanese politicians were too ignorant of military and technical matters to refute the nuclear umbrella myth..."[9] Ishihara is referring to the value of the American nuclear shield during all the cold war years, and is explaining Japanese innocence in world affairs. That's hard to accept.

What we are witnessing in the 1990s is nothing less than the renaissance of the Japanese imperialist policies of the 1930s. Nothing hurt Japanese-American relations worse than the United States' 1970s rapprochement with China. Japan felt that it had a proprietary interest in China. China was its market and in its sphere of influence. The United States should have had the sense to stay out, or at least, to have advised the Japanese in advance that it wanted to open relations with China. In Japanese eyes, opening diplomatic relations with China, without the proper introductions from Japan, was an unforgivable sin. The United States should have accepted and bowed to Japan's sovereignty. [10]

For twenty-five years prior to World War II, Japan believed that it alone had the right to advise China. Japan rejected every program from the "Open Door" policy to the "Integrity of China" policy. The Nine-Power Treaty, the Pact of Paris, and the Council of Ten were all dismissed. And, at the Washington Conference, Japan rejected the notion that any Westerner could examine Sino-Japanese relations. In the 1990s, Japan's commitment to its dominant Asian role is as much a part of its policy as it was in the 1930s.

Japan also has an enormous need for the natural resources available in Siberia. In negotiations with the Russians, Japan proposed that in return for the four northern Kurile Islands, it would finance the economic development of Siberia.

The Japanese seem to assume that the Russians are too dimwitted to understand that Japan desperately needs Siberia's raw materials and the space, especially if it is to reduce its dependence on the United States and Europe. The old Greater East Asia Co-Prosperity Sphere from the 1930s is being resurrected. What Japan could not win by war, it is about to win by economic means. The message from Morita and Ishihara and many others makes clear that Japan seeks world power.

It is important that Americans and Europeans understand that Japan plans to become the dominant economic force in the world. Obviously, this can't be done without displacing the Western powers that have been holding the primary economic positions. Japan's strategy begins with the economic conquest of Asia, especially Korea, Singapore and Taiwan where it began with its earliest overseas investments, and therefore has its deepest economic penetration. According to Morita, "It might be too much to say that they [other Asian countries] developed thanks to the Japanese economy and industrial technologies, but I believe we contributed to them in such a way that contributed to their prosperity. From now on, Japan will need to take a major role in Asia."[11]

Clearly, Japan has already taken a dominant role. The following are Japan's investments in millions of U.S. dollars for 1986/87, and a three-year cumulative investment figure for several countries of the Far East and Oceania.[12] The last column shows Japanese investments during the first six months of 1990 alone.

These figures reveal recent direct investments only. They do not indicate the number of long-term development loans, which are not always made public, or joint marketing ventures, which are a significant part of Japanese investment strategy. Consequently, these figures do not tell the whole story. For example, in 1965, as part of Japan's reconciliation with South Korea, Korea was awarded a 500 million dollar package of grants and loans. It bought Japan an important interest in South Korea's leading corporations. It also brought the Koreans into close economic association with the Japanese *keiretsus*, which are cooperating business groups in Japan.

JAPANESE FOREIGN INVESTMENT IN THE FAR EAST AND OCEANIA

	86/87	3 YRS	6 MONTHS, 1990*
Australia	$881	($1,454)	n.a.
Hong Kong	$502	($1,045)	$1,059
Indonesia	$250	($1,032)	$434
Singapore	$302	($866)	$360
So. Korea	$436	($677)	$140
Taiwan	$291	($470)	n.a.
Malaysia	n.a.	n.a.	$368

* Source: Ministry of Finance. Yen 136 = U.S. $1.00

Japan's five billion dollar loan package to China, announced in 1990, is a more significant figure than its direct investments in China. Generally, when the Japanese invest, they prefer either making low levels of direct investment sufficient only to gain access to foreign technology, or loans that will generate export opportunities and repay the initial capital outlay over time.

Such shrewd policies have helped build Japan's empire — an empire that poses a grave threat to the United States. If ever there was a time for the U.S. to be cautious and to prepare itself, it is now. Japanese rage exists because Japan believes that the United States is standing in the way of its growth. The West hears rumblings about its unfair trade laws, but is seldom allowed to see the depth of Japanese feelings. Yet, the United States must also recognize that Japan has access to our most classified documents, and has friends in high places in the U.S. government. They know what the United States is doing and how ill prepared Americans are to combat them. The Western world is oddly vulnerable to economic attack, where militarily it is almost perfectly safe.

The Japanese see themselves as the last and best civilization in the world. They see themselves as having borne the brunt of Western avarice and duplicity. They don't suffer from Western-style egocentrism, but rather from ethnocentrism to a degree unknown in the West.

Japan has the brains and the growing resource base to accomplish any and all of its goals. It is critical for the United States and Europe to rebuild manufacturing and industrial bases. It is essential that the West understands that Japan's plan is long-term. Sometimes it seems indeed that Westerners can't think ahead more than twenty minutes, as Morita claims, and that is exactly what the Japanese are counting on. Japan believes that the West will never recover economic dominance. It believes that the West is already lost and is just too stupid to surrender.

CHAPTER TWO

KATA: The Proper Form, Rules

One of the interesting vignettes in *The Japan That Can Say No* details the monthly meetings of the Prime Minister's cabinet. Like many meetings in America's corporate boardrooms and government offices, they are often boring, and the participants find themselves fighting to stay awake. The Japanese Prime Minister's meetings tend to be dominated by reports from the Bureau Chief of the Economic Planning Agency and from the Governor of the Bank of Japan. These kinds of reports are usually dry and not very informative. Page after page of numbers tend to get tedious. Yet, when Ishihara suggested that these meetings be cancelled, Chief Cabinet Secretary Keizo Obuchi claimed that the meetings were essential, even if not everybody paid attention. They could not afford to slight any L.D.P. officials who attend regularly.

And so, every month a nearly identical report is presented. The Bureau Chief of the Economic Planning Agency says the same things he said the month before, namely that the magnitude of Japan's balance of trade is shrinking. And, for a brief period in 1989, it did appear that Japan's rate of export growth was slackening. But, according to Ishihara, all that the ministers do is underline this passage of the report in red, then wait for the next item on the agenda. In effect, he complains, by their silence, they are accepting that it is okay for business to be failing. In reality, business wasn't failing. It was just experiencing a short period of slower than normal growth. But even a period of slow growth causes extreme anxiety among many Japanese.

This phenomenon of acceptance is known in Japan as *kata*, a kind of blind adherence to the proper way of doing things. Each minister has his own portfolio: Agriculture, foreign affairs, transportation, etc. In order not to appear impolite, each minister tends to say nothing about subjects outside his own portfolio, except to routinely endorse what other ministers report or propose. Rules of Japanese culture say that one should obey one's superiors. Great store is set by getting along with each other. Peace is best. In his area, each minister is the highest authority, so his word is taken as law in most cases. It is understood as a cultural function that the minister will not endorse a point of view unless it has been reached with the consensus of his department.

A similar philosophy is evident in the United States, but with tragically different and divisive results. As it might be defined in America, *kata* is a blind allegiance to your leader, a person, or an idea, rather than to a form or procedure. It is accomplished in business by senior managements' exclusionary tactics and power blocs. Employees are rarely consulted and consensus is seldom sought. The plan originates at, or near, the top, and is later promulgated throughout the lower organization. Lower managers and their workers are expected to trust the wisdom from the top and to go along with company policy, whatever it may be.

Power blocs exist in Japan, but they are usually formed like equilateral triangles with a solid base of support. The Japanese power bloc is the result of consensus derived from the participation of people lower in the organization. In America, the power bloc is all too often shaped like a triangle standing on its point. These blocs often represent the power a single industry has in shaping government policy. One example is the oil industry's ability to dictate the nation's energy strategy.

How many Western companies encourage a middle-level manager to voice opposition to a proposed company policy? How many are even invited to the planning meeting? And other than to ask polite, clarifying questions, how many American marketing executives will seriously challenge the production department's plan for a new factory or its location? In America, these are highly sensitive areas involving competing territorial interests. There is almost no cross-departmental discussion in most corporations on the larger conceptual issues. Namely, should a new factory be built and, if so, where? Instead, the various departments are asked only to contribute bits and pieces of information on demographics, taxes, and transportation. The people who do the work never learn the outcome of their efforts. The organization's top echelon makes the decisions, and when convenient, lets the rest of the company know its decision.

Especially in larger corporations, the old Yankee Trader spirit has died. Employee motivation has become a whole area of business in itself. Americans used to be such great salesmen in the days when team-building entrepreneurs were dominant. Today, American business is run by MBAs with career goals and tennis dates.

Ishihara, however, is upset with the Japanese philosophy of *kata*. Speaking out on themes that might cause other people embarrassment, he appears to be a maverick in his own country. Ishihara complained to Seiroku Kajiyama, the Minister for Home Affairs, that if this trend continues, Japan will lose its competitive edge. He is tired of hearing reports on negative trends and of having setbacks and losses routinely accepted without complaint or a plan for improvement. He is afraid that in an effort to keep face, to preserve a proper form to the meetings, the Japanese are altering their values.

In truth, Ishihara has very little to fear. As late as the third calendar quarter of 1991, all the major economic reports showed that Japan was enjoying the longest period of economic expansion since World War II. Only in the fourth quarter of 1991 did the Japanese economy slow to a two-tenths of a percentage point drop in G.N.P. from the previous quarter. The Ministry of Finance had predicted that all Japanese pretax corporate profits would grow at 3.5 percent in fiscal 1991, compared to 2.5 percent in 1990, and it saw revenues growing at 5.0 percent. Gross national product actually grew at a 4.5 percent rate during 1990 and 3.0 percent in 1991. The Ministry also reported that Japan's surplus with the rest of the world for November 1991 was 7.26 billion dollars, a 330 percent increase over the previous year. Japan's current account surplus for fiscal 1991 should exceed 100 billion dollars—double the year before.[1]

These figures are just as robust as any others that Japan has seen in recent years, and they still reflect a continuing healthy growth. Japan's 1991 fourth quarter G.N.P. slowdown is more a sign of economic trouble in Europe and America than it is of any inherent problem at home. Yet a recession in two of its markets is probably enough to take the steam out of the Japanese expansion.

The Japanese economy was led by domestic demand in the early quarters of fiscal 1989, but industrial output from mines and factories had begun to surge ahead by early 1990. Based on 1985 production levels, these industries were about 25 percent ahead in mid-1990 and the outlook continues to be positive.[2] Japan, in 1992, is still performing better than any other industrialized nation.

Japan's economy is vaulting into the 1990s on a head of steam provided by a resurgent export business and steady growth in the home market. This fact should be noted critically in the United States. Japanese trade surpluses are rising again, and the brunt of this burden is being felt by America. The January-March 1990 quarter represents the first time since the end of 1984 that foreign demand contributed more to Japan's G.N.P. growth than domestic demand.[3]

Part of this renewed export growth is due to the strength of other Asian economies. Asia has now become as important a market for Japan as the United States. Europe, too, has been a larger customer in recent quarters, and this has helped to offset the slowdown in the growth of demand from the United States. The only cloud on Japan's economic horizon is a growing labor shortage, which may in time have some impact on wages and output.

An interesting piece of information was mentioned in one of the Prime Minister's cabinet meetings in a presentation called the Maekawa Report. It stated that Japan's economic and industrial structure is turning away from heavy manufacturing and primary industries to cleaner, more knowledge-intensive businesses. This development had actually been planned by the Ministry of International Trade and Industry in the 1970s, and so it did not come as a surprise. However, the industrial base of Japan has always been thought of in positive terms by Japanese society. It is referred to as *jukochodai*, meaning not only massive and strong, but something aesthetically admirable, as is a sumo wrestler, for example.

Many Japanese leaders are concerned that these newer industries, being lighter and smaller, may not embody Japan's cultural sense. It is not Japanese to avoid work which dirties the hands. Japan's leaders fear for a nation that has forgotten how to sweat. They agree that brain work is important and respectable, but also feel that it is not the foundation of a nation. They are not questioning MITI's 1970s plan for Japan's expansion into semiconductors and other computer-related businesses, but are suggesting that future efforts ought to be in meatier pursuits. Heavy industry is necessary for economic survival.In fact, there is a kind of muscle flexing going on in Japan these days. It is still just a wistful sort of daydreaming for many people, but it exists, and it should be recognized. The Japanese are justly proud of their accomplishments. They have money and power as they have never had before. They are thinking more often of how things ought to be, *kata*. And the spirit of *bushido*, the way of the warrior, is coming more and more alive. Though that spirit may not always be warlike, it is a Japan-first philosophy. It is the same philosophy that allowed Japan to believe that their occupation of Manchuria in the 1930s was for the good of all.

This self-righteousness is a critical aspect of any analysis and interpretation of things Japanese. The Japanese have a vision of what is and is not Japanese, and of what is and is not socially or economically acceptable. They have a vision of where each person belongs in society on a hierarchical scale that exists nowhere on paper.

Ishihara is afraid that if the Japanese forget their heritage of manual labor they will evolve into a head-heavy sub-species. Japan's poor performance at the Seoul Olympics worries him, because it indicates the loss of the physical abilities which Ishihara believes are the true source of a nation's strength.

The Ministry of International Trade and Industry shares Ishihara's concerns. In fact, over the years they have helped to establish his vision. MITI's vision in past decades saw Japan as world leader in steel, automobiles, semiconductors and consumer electronics. This vision has now become a national economic war plan and any American who works, or has worked, in these Japanese-dominated industries should understand how this vision materialized. In 1990, MITI envisioned a "mellow society," where the aged could live comfortably. They foresaw larger homes for workers, where the dinner table would resume an important place in Japanese culture. Of course, this could only be possible if the Japanese have more living space for their population.

Theoretically, land acquisition is not a necessary part of the MITI dream. The Japanese could always build taller apartment buildings to accomodate their growing population. However, a problem occurs when these people leave their buildings. It takes a long time to go anywhere in Japan. The streets and public transportation systems are clogged with people. Japan is the most densely populated nation on earth. For this reason, the problems of congestion can only be solved with territory.

MITI's vision for the 1990s is one of territorial expansion, although not necessarily by military force.

During those years when MITI did not lead the Japanese people in their vision, and it has had its ups and downs, its directors became followers. But, MITI has never been completely out of step. It has never erred in the consensus vision, only in its timing or in minor tactical aspects.

MITI's function in Japan is far too important to be allowed to diverge significantly, or for long, from the national will. Its role is to prevent excessive competition within the nation and to support strategically important industries. MITI has the power to create markets and to buy products. It can force mergers of Japanese corporations to achieve monopolistic efficiency and to defeat foreign competitors. It protects domestic technology and forbids the licensing of Japanese inventions that might be useful to another country.

By utilizing these powers, MITI has effectively ruined the dynamic random access memory (DRAM) semiconductor business for the United States. The whole field of supercomputers is now on the verge of becoming, if not a Japanese monopoly, at least a Japanese-controlled market. The Japanese will produce the semiconductors that make the supercomputers work, and therefore will have them first. Hitachi has already announced a DRAM chip with a 64 megabit capacity that will be ready for the market by 1994. One tiny silicon wafer will offer enough memory to contain two long novels. It is 16 times more powerful than what IBM, and others, are currently offering.

Japanese dominance in the fields of electronics and semiconductors also affects world defense strategies. In Chapter Eleven, "*Hara*, A Centralized Force," I will discuss Japan's military development plans. For now, it should be noted that Shinichiro Ohta, MITI's head of aircraft and ordinance division, says that MITI doesn't have any national (aerospace) goals. The reality appears to be otherwise. One of Japan's major goals for the 1990s is to improve space and aviation technology. The evidence is overwhelming, and the already recorded joint ventures and mergers and purchases only confirm this point. Japan's current plan to support research in jet engines, and to support these industries with tax breaks, only serves to advertise the truth of the matter.

Ishihara has chided the United States and the former Soviet Union over their nuclear arms reduction treaties. These arms reductions, he claims, were not motivated by any sense of danger, nor were the Russians and Americans acting with any sense of human morality.

The real reason for the treaties—and here Ishihara speaks with more than a little truth—is that all missiles, whether mid-range or ICBM, are guided in their targeting accuracy by high precision computers. Nuclear missiles have multiple warheads, some of which are dummies to confuse the enemy, but some are real. All the warheads reenter the atmosphere in tumbling patterns, run sideways, and follow otherwise complicated paths. They land on their targets with an accuracy of one second of latitude and longitude.

The targets, reinforced concrete structures that go 150 to 200 feet deep into the earth, are the enemy's missile silos. Unless a direct hit is scored, the missiles are undisturbed. Earthquakes are more of a danger to these missiles than are enemy nuclear bombs. (The official translation reverses this point.)[4] In the event of war, a direct hit is vital or the effort is wasted, because the enemy is then able to launch a counterstrike.

Current technology allows Russian missiles to strike fairly often within a 60 meter (200 feet) area, while American missiles can usually hit within 15 meters (50 feet). Both sides acknowledge that some enemy missiles would always escape. To be assured of enemy missile destruction, a direct hit has to be made. This is why the former Soviet Union developed such huge mega-tonnage weapons, up to ten times larger than U.S. warheads. It makes up somewhat for their less-accurate guidance systems.

Programming a direct hit calls for an enormously complex missile trajectory and an extremely sophisticated source of artificial intelligence. While the United States is the leader in fourth generation semiconductors, and has the know-how to create the fifth generation one-megabit semiconductors, it fails when it comes to production. Today, according to Ishihara, only Japan has the advanced production management skills and the manufacturing capability in place to produce these new generation chips. Hitachi and Texas Instruments are working jointly to develop a four-megabit semiconductor, but when it comes time for production, the odds favor a Japanese venture.

In a nutshell, if Japanese semiconductors are not used, neither the Americans nor the Russians can hit each other's targets. This is the point that Ishihara is making in his book. Disarmament is the only rational option left to the nuclear powers. They cannot build the core of their national defense structures around Japanese-controlled technology. Continued military expansion becomes senseless when they each have to rely on Japan to sell them the necessary chips. The chips are vital to nearly every phase of a modern electronic war. They are used in almost every weapons system from missile guidance and propulsion to naval defense efforts and sonar tracking to battlefield logistics.

Up to this point, Ishihara's vision could reasonably be taken as an intellectual exercise in the analysis of world defense postures. However, he doesn't leave off there. In an unveiled threat to the United States, he warns that if Japan sold these chips to America's enemies and withheld them from the United States, Japan could completely upset the entire world balance of power. Then, in a bid pandering to Japanese fear of the United States, Ishihara warns of a possible U.S. reoccupation of Japan. But in finishing his thought, he soothes Japanese nerves by noting that there is no way that the Western powers can catch up to Japan. As each year goes by, the West, including the new Eastern European countries, will become more dependent on Japanese technology.

As if to underscore this point, the United States Department of Commerce, in a report released on June 10, 1990, said that Japan could surpass the U.S. in production of electronic goods by the early 1990s. This was hardly news. Most Americans thought Japan was already far ahead in this field.

John McPhee, a co-author of the Commerce report, said, "Except in software and medical equipment, the U.S. has been losing market share in all products since 1984." The United States still produces over 180 billion dollars worth of electronics yearly, but if current trends continue, the Japanese will surpass that level by 1994.

Japanese electronics companies are growing at a rate of 27-28 percent per year, while their American counterparts are sluggishly growing at rates closer to 10 percent. Equally important is the fact that of the top five corporations to receive the most electronics patents as long ago as 1987, the first three were Japanese: Canon, Hitachi and Toshiba. General Electric and N.V. Philips of the Netherlands were fourth and fifth, respectively.

To hammer home his feelings about Japan's growing importance in world affairs, Ishihara cites a classified report on electronic engineering prepared by the Pentagon's Defense Science Board that reveals the U.S.'s sense of crisis.

The report states that a Japan left unchallenged will prevent the United States from regaining the lead in electronics and semiconductor technology. Ishihara agrees that the report is accurate in assessing the relative areas of U.S. weaknesses and Japanese strengths. This report is so confidential, he informs us, that it has been seen only by the President of the United States and a few of his closest advisors — and by Ishihara. If it were seen by the general public, it would certainly raise a commotion, he speculates.

Over the years, Japan and most of the free world have become dependent on America's nuclear umbrella and military strength. But now, with the change of war to an electronic phenomenon, with semiconductors being the key element, Japan finds itself in a new position. Namely, how serious is Japan's need for American military assistance? This is a position that is discussed more and more in Japan these days.

With a new balance of power emerging as a result of Japanese dominance of semiconductors, a reevaluation of all defense strategies is on the table. The long-run implications are staggering, and it becomes important to understand how the United States came to this position.

Mass production of semiconductors depends on having a mass market. Few people in the United States government seem to comprehend this critical point. Far too many elected officials in Washington support free trade only because they do not want to be branded with the old Smoot-Hawley tarbrush of restrictive tariffs. What they fail to realize is that Smoot-Hawley raised tariffs indiscriminately, against friend and foe alike, making America an isolated fortress. That was not the answer then, and it is not the answer now. But it has always been acceptable, and is today almost universally the practice, for nations to protect industries that are critical to their well-being. Is it really necessary that the United States be more holy than France, Italy or Germany in matters of trade policy? Count the Japanese cars on European roads in comparison to those in the United States, or the number of VCRs, and then ask: Why is America so tolerant?

Japan was quick to see a use for semiconductors in rice cookers and other household appliances. In fact, the Japanese saw the applications for a wide range of products before the United States did. This gave them a market both to support their production facilities and to be able to afford the development of the higher density chips. Even though it invented semiconductors, America has now been preempted in the semiconductor market, certainly in the mass production bulk business and in the manufacture of higher density, extremely sophisticated chips. Americans are far too quick to license their inventions to foreign production, and far too slow to develop home uses for their technology. A little government interference in the licensing of inventions, and time for reflection by the corporate developers, might save Americans a lot of trouble. The result in the case of the semiconductor market was that the U.S. manufacturers got a late start in production, and since then have been largely kept to niche markets. Frankly, it is unlikely that the United States will ever catch up to Japan.

The classified Science Board report, as cited by Ishihara, says that "America's semiconductor industry is losing its ability to compete with Japan. There is a strong relationship between production and marketing end uses, and America has lost enormous market share in all sizes of semiconductors. It is out of business on the larger versions and is completely dependent on Japan for the one-megabit chips. The Commission task team finds this situation unacceptable to national security."[5] Well, at least somebody finally recognizes the situation and wrote a report. But it makes you wonder.

Doesn't anybody review Pentagon purchase orders? Didn't somebody notice ten years ago the growing dependence of the U.S. military on Japanese sources? Is it so hard to talk to elected government officials? Wasn't there one Congressperson who would have listened had the message been brought to his or her attention?

The problem is that the United States does not have a national plan or direction. There is no sense of where the country is headed. There are no common goals. It would be hard to imagine a modern corporation trying to do business today without a marketing plan, but this is exactly what the United States is doing. As a result, American government employees don't have yardsticks by which to measure the progress of their departments. They don't know what is wasteful and counterproductive. They are good people trying to do their best, but they don't know where to direct their energies. It is up to the elected government to tell them. America needs a leader today as much as it did when Franklin D. Roosevelt was president. Like him or not, Roosevelt knew where he was going.

Ishihara rails at the United States for its crisis attitude. The Americans fear that Japan might sell too many semiconductors to its enemies, thereby causing the United States to lose a significant military advantage. He says that if a European country had the lead in semiconductors, there would be no concern. He raises the old "yellow peril" flag, and says that only because an Oriental country has the lead is America in such a state of hysteria. Ishihara defends Toshiba's sale of restricted, electronically controlled machine tools to what was then the Soviet Union, and castigates the United States Congress for penalizing Toshiba, citing this as an unlawful restraint of trade.

Ishihara, furthermore, points out that though the United States has the knowledge to make one-megabit semiconductors it does not have the ability. Sophisticated semiconductors can only be made in Japan at this point. The United States has neither the skilled technicians, nor the shop workers, nor the machinery to go into production. Equally important, the United States does not have the qualified management teams. Even if America set up shop today in a cheap labor market, it could not catch up to Japan. Japan is at least five years ahead, and the gap is widening daily.

Only a small part of this claim is bravado. The United States has performed some herculean tasks in the past, and no doubt could repeat the performance. But, it is becoming more difficult daily, and it is certainly true that the U.S. could never catch up to the Japanese without government protection of its markets and development assistance.

Even basic research is now being compromised, because there are so many research phases that require high density semiconductors. It takes a supercomputer to produce a greater supercomputer. This is a fact of technological development. In other words, the longer the gap is allowed to widen between Japan and the United States, the more impossible it will be for America to catch up.

Supercomputers have become central to military strength and are therefore central to national power. Ishihara offers the example of designing a Mach 2 airplane. A regular computer might take 40 years to compute the stress and propulsion variables, but the newer super-computers could do these analyses in one year. It follows that since Japan owns virtually 100 percent of the one-megabit semiconductor market, Japan, in a real sense, has become a world power.

There are several Japanese companies working on supercomputer development in competition with International Business Machines and Cray Research. The NEC Corporation, though a small player in this field, recently unveiled a remarkable new machine called the ACOS 3800. It can compute 100 million instructions per second (mips) on one processor, and 500 mips with six processors. NEC's biggest flaw is a lack of software compatibility, but still its technology development has to be recognized. Hitachi and Fujitsu are also in the running with serious competition for the American manufacturers.

Japanese strategic planning includes expanded participation in the world market, especially in China and Siberia. In the continuing negotiations with the Russians, Japan still withholds the carrot of development funding and material assistance for Siberia until Japan's northern Kurile Islands are returned. But it is only a matter of time before Russia's need will overcome its reluctance. Just before the July 1990 meeting of the Group of Seven in Houston, Texas, Prime Minister Kaifu secured a promise from President George Bush, that, in spite of the Tiananmen Square massacre, the United States would not object to Japan's renewal of five billion dollars' worth of aid payments to China.

It is an article of faith in Japan that it is the natural trading partner for all Pacific Rim countries, including Russia and its bordering countries. The Japanese have made it a point to position themselves in the forefront of all major new technological developments. And with this position firmly in hand, they should be able to control trade in the region.

Superconductors, for example, will be an important next generation development option for Japan. Germany is the only other country with a potential for competition in this area, but the theoretical base of Japanese technology is already far ahead of them. As Germany is giving up supercondutor research, Japan is overcoming the major obstacles that the Germans considered too expensive to surmount. The Americans, meanwhile, were content with the invention only and then mostly gave up on the idea.

To cite an example, the German magnetic train has never been able to achieve a levitation of more than eight millimeters. However, Japan's Maglev superconducting linear railcar manages a levitation of 10 centimeters (four inches) and reaches speeds of 500 kilometers (310 miles) per hour.

This type of sophisticated technology does not exist anywhere else in the world. If the decision-makers of Japanese business and government can work together on this new technology, it will open a future without rivals; all the rest of Asia will be forced into the Japanese camp by default.

The Japanese HSST Corporation has already made a start in this direction by agreeing with Russia to build a 20-mile rail link between central Moscow and Sheremetyevo International Airport. HSST will sell the technology to build these high speed, magnetically levitated trains that float on air rather than run on wheels. Construction was scheduled to begin in 1992 and should be completed in 1996 at a cost of about 610 million dollars, if it actually goes ahead.

In an even bolder venture, Mitsubishi Heavy Industries has just christened a 185-ton ship, the Yamato No. 1. It will be the first vessel to use superconductivity for propulsion. The Kobe shipyard is likely to reap some significant new business from this daring stroke. Just imagine the speed potential and the quietness of ships that no longer have to rely on old-fashioned propulsion systems. America's entire submarine fleet could become obsolete within a decade.

There is a group in Japan called the *Jiyu Shaki Kenkyu-kai*, or Free Society Research Association. It consists of leading businessmen and politicians, and meets several times a year. This organization took special note of former United States Secretary of State Henry Kissinger's prediction that Japan would become a military superpower, though not by building Yamato class battle-ships or by installing ICBMs. Kissinger is said to have pointed out that no matter how many space stations the Soviet Union and the United States build, and no matter how much money America spends on B1 and B2 bombers and SDI (star wars satel-lites), both countries are dependent on Japanese technology.[6]

With these facts before the nation, the feeling in Japan is that the people are being called upon to proceed boldly to build a new culture for themselves based on advanced technology. The Japanese are being urged not to lag in this effort. Japan's leaders feel that they must finally shake off the constraints imposed upon them by post-War American occupation. A revolution in the Japanese consciousness is being called for. They are expected to remember *giri*, their duty to their emperor, country, company and family, in that order.

The Japanese press has reported extensively on the upheavals in the former Soviet Union under Mikhail Gorbachev, the Chinese Cultural Revolution, and on the American social changes brought about by the Vietnam War experience. Ishihara believes that such social revolution should happen in Japan, too. Japan, he complains, is the only country in the world that has not felt some need for extensive reform since the end of World War II. He wants the politicians to get motivated to institute some reforms, and to stop doing things as they have always been done. In short, Ishihara wants Japan to recognize its potential for world power status.

It must be frustrating being Japanese in the 1990s. *Kata* dictates international acceptance of the Japanese in the world power structure. Japan has become wealthy and exercises an economic power unknown since the United States held the same position just after World War II. Yet, the Japanese believe the world snubs Tokyo.

CHAPTER THREE

America In Decline

"Ten minute planning." That is how Akio Morita (C.O.B., Sony) characterizes future planning in the United States. The frequently heard opinion from Japan is that Americans have never been able to see beyond today's bank balance, the next accounting period, or this quarter. According to Morita, the entire concept of forward thinking is alien to the impatient, uncivilized Americans.

In the Japanese version of *The Japan That Can Say No*, Morita simplifies Ishihara's message by suggesting that the gist of it is an emphasis on the importance of industrial production. Morita is a world traveler with business interests on every continent except Antarctica. In all of his discussions and debates, one point has made itself clear to him. "The Americans have forgotten the importance of manufacturing and production," he says.

Looking at the decline of so many American industries over the past 20 years, it certainly seems true that contemporary America is incapable of strategic thinking. How else can one explain the loss of so many manufacturing jobs in the United States?

When World War II ended, the United States had the most skilled labor force in the world and the greatest number of factories in operation. In 1950, the U.S. manufacturing sector employed 38.9 percent of the American workforce (excluding agriculture); the construction business six percent; and mining, 2.3 percent. A total of 47.2 percent of working Americans were involved in the process of adding value to products and commodities.[1]

By 1989, the total number of workers in the above categories had fallen to 28.2 percent. Manufacturing had 21.6 percent of that share; construction, 5.8 percent; and mining, 0.8 percent. This is an employment decline of 40 percent in the vital industrial sectors that build the real wealth of nations. By and large, these workers have been absorbed by the retail and wholesale trades, finance, insurance and real estate companies, and by other service operations. Needless to say, real salaries and wages have been declining in direct proportion to the shift in employment venues. The best wages have always been paid by businesses that add value to products.

These are startling numbers that should have every man and woman in the country up in arms demanding a change in America's industrial policies. Unfortunately, Americans are a politically lazy people, self-satisfied when employed and uncaring of less fortunate neighbors. Americans, like the Japanese, tend to believe what they read in the newspapers. For example, many Americans believed Henry Tashima, President of the Minolta Camera Company, Osaka, Japan, when he wrote that "America is still the richest country in the world...that manufacturing continues to account for about 24 percent of the United States' G.N.P. as it has since the 1960s."[2] The source of his data was not cited in the article, and the newspaper did not correct him. He was dead wrong. However, it's comforting to be told that all is well, that it's just a matter of America's regaining its confidence. But hidden behind Tashima's words of reassurance is the *Keidanren's* multimillion dollar public relations campaign that placates the U.S. and convinces it to accept all things Japanese, especially automobiles, electronics, textiles and cameras.

A visit to any major American industrial city—be it Boston, New York, Philadelphia, Pittsburgh, Cleveland, Akron, Detroit, Gary or Chicago—will demonstrate the utter waste and futility of America's trade policy over the past 40 years. Whole industries have died or are ailing: Shoes and textiles, iron and steel, automobiles and rubber, electronics and appliances. Jobs that used to support families and pay taxes and that created wealth and hope for the future have been lost. These factories are now rusting hulks, monuments to both industrial mismanagement and idiotic devotion to free trade.

Even when it seemed that America was at last fighting back and making some headway in the struggle to keep its manufacturers afloat, it was really losing. Economic life in the United States has for so long been an illusion of smoke and mirrors that it is now hard to distinguish chimera from reality. "In the period that most people would probably identify as the best of times," wrote Kirk Johnson, a writer on business topics, "roughly 1984 to 1988—New England's economic base, especially manufacturing, was already in decline. The six-state region lost nearly 56,000 manufacturing jobs in 1986 alone, according to DRI/McGraw Hill, an economics consulting firm in Massachusetts."[3]

However, in this same period, the region gained 166,000 jobs in service and information-processing industries. This misled people into believing that happy days were here again. "What was happening, economists say, was the equivalent of foregoing a balanced if boring meal in favor of a plate full of candy bars. Manufacturing jobs make an economy grow, albeit slowly."[4] Service industries support manufacturing and can be economically volatile. Real estate, retailing and other service jobs tend to spark booms that are short-lived. That is what has happened not only in New England, but in countless other communities throughout America.

In September 1990, it was announced that Cincinnati Milacron, the last major manufacturer of heavy robots in America, had sold its business to a Swiss company. The only odd thing about this sale is that, for a change, the buyer was not Japanese. The biggest buyers of America's high-tech industries are usually Japanese companies. Robots and machine tools, such as those produced by Cincinnati Milacron, are essential to America's, and any other nation's, manufacturing health. The country that controls America's tooling industries also controls its manufacturing future.

In the summer of 1990, New York City lost 34,000 jobs, according to the Bureau of Labor Statistics. 5,200 lost jobs were in manufacturing; 5,600 in construction; and the rest in finance, service and trade. In the past decade, the only consistent job growth in this major American city has been in government employment, real estate, insurance and retailing. The annual loss of manufacturing and construction jobs has been a plague on this metropolitan economy. Nor is New York alone. Every major city in the United States has seen more and more job losses in manufacturing and construction, especially over the last decade.

The import target for the federal government's Voluntary Restraint Program in the steel industry is 19.1 percent of consumption in any one year. It is hard to believe that this amounts to over 1,500,000 tons of steel imported into the United States every month of the year. The United States, in contrast, exports only 350,000 tons of steel every month.[5] This situation exists in spite of the fact that steel is heavy, and transportation costs are high. These figures reveal the continuing deterioration of another of America's basic, core industries. Because of unregulated foreign competition and gross mismanagement of its companies, this industry has already lost tens of thousands of workers, and the trend seems certain to continue unless a fired-up U.S. Congress takes action.

Back in the late 1950s, a ten million car production year was a good, reasonable goal for the U.S. automobile industry. Since then, another 90 million people have been added to the population, but annual domestic car production has fallen to levels of seven to eight million units per year, depending on the state of the economy. Japan has seized the market of low-priced cars while making extraordinary inroads on the mid-priced market. Germany, meanwhile, has taken over the high-priced market of prestige vehicles.

It's not that American labor is too expensive. On the contrary, compared with manufacturing nations, especially to its major trading partners, U.S. wages are competitive, as can be seen in the following chart.[6] But, in spite of the fact that the American worker puts in as many hours and is paid at comparable rates, the U.S. market share continues to decline.

AVERAGE 1990 HOURLY COMPENSATION IN MANUFACTURING (INCLUDING BENEFITS)

West Germany	$21.30
Canada	15.94
France	15.25
United States	14.83
Japan	12.84
South Korea	4.16
Taiwan	3.98
Mexico	1.85

American blue-collar workers have been feeling the pinch on wages for many years. "From 1980 to 1990, after adjusting for inflation, the wages of blue-collar workers fell by 6.3 percent, while white-collar salaries rose 3.9 percent."[7] Even the long Reagan recovery did not halt the decline in manufacturing wages.

Toyota is building another plant in Kentucky to double its production capacity, and the people of that region are thrilled. They should be—a production job in a Japanese automobile plant is a lot healthier than part-time coal mining. What's hard to swallow is that General Motors, Ford and Chrysler have allowed it to happen. An uncooperative, uncomprehending government is only a part of the automobile industry's problem. To this day, the Detroit auto makers are still feeding the Japanese with increasing orders for more parts and automobiles. The outcome of this trend is as predictable as cancer. Chrysler will soon be defunct again (Lee Iacocca is leaving not a day too soon), and General Motors will accelerate its diversification plan in a desperate search for industries where it doesn't have to compete with anybody. When the Japanese finally control America's basic industries, pricing will be done by their cartels, out of reach of the Justice Department and American law. Then Japan will begin in earnest to collect upon the debts America owes them.

The new General Motors Saturn plant in Spring Hill, Tennessee, was inaugurated with a lot of hoopla in October 1990. It incorporates many of the manufacturing procedures that have worked so well in Japan and that should work well here. It also appears, a little more than a year later, that the G.M. management, at least in this one plant, is trying to maintain a decent working relationship with its production workers. It is important to America's manufacturing future that this plant succeed, because it is a trail-blazing model.

The General Accounting Office said that the Japanese car manufacturers in the United States had cost 36,000 American jobs in 1988 and 1989.[8] Their factories require fewer workers and use fewer American parts. So, while Kentuckians might rejoice in getting the new Toyota plant, they should also remember that the plant does not indicate any new rosy sign for the rest of U.S. car manufacturers.

In a report issued by the Bureau of Labor Statistics, the earnings of American nonsupervisory workers rose from $136 per week in 1972 to $359 a week in 1991. However, it was all an illusion because inflation rose faster. Real wages actually fell 19 percent. Workers in the United States can only buy four-fifths of what they could afford twenty years ago. Its the major reason why most households are now supported by two wage-earners rather than one. Yet, in this same period, American labor productivity was improving an average 2.1 percent a year. American industries are hard-pressed by low-wage overseas competitors, and its workers are forced to compete with Korean, Chinese and Malayan labor at wages far beneath what it costs to live in the United States. At some point, the U.S. government will have to recognize this fact and deal with it.

Unfortunately, it is not just manufacturing jobs that are being lost today. Already, the trend has broadened to include the finance, real estate and insurance industries. Economies built on boom-time industries such as real estate have always been volatile in terms of employment. The failed savings and loan institutions cost the economy thousands of jobs, not to mention lost capital. The commercial banking industry, too, has fallen on hard times. It has lost market share to the growing number of foreign banks operating in American financial centers, and made bad loans to real estate speculators as well as to unstable foreign countries. The result is predictable to anybody but a banker—earnings are down and layoffs are up. Bank of America fired 10,000 employees; Citicorp, 9,000, and Chemical Bank, 6,200. Chase Manhattan dropped 5,000 employees, or 12 percent of its workforce.

The same pattern can be seen in the insurance industry which is burdened with overvalued real estate and high-claims payout rates on automobile and accident insurance policies. A low-wage future built on part-time service work and minimum skilled assembly jobs is on the horizon for many Americans. A no-wage future is more likely if the person happens to be African-American. Jesse Jackson may not be the smoothest politician ever to cross the American scene, but at least, he is not the radical alternative that is growing up in places like Milwaukee and Detroit. It is foolish for the white community to ignore Jackson, and other moderate leaders, especially when these leaders are still willing to work within the system.

There is a lot at stake for the United States in the next few years, and it is important that Americans are aware of the potential for disaster. That the United States has not already been torn apart by street riots is a testimony to the patience and law-abiding nature of its population. But, this is not a condition that Americans can count on forever. The homeless in the United States have never been counted. Even the Census Department admits its failure.

According to Ted Houghton, Assistant Director for Advocacy at the New York Coalition for the Homeless, on any one night in the United States there are about 600,000 people who are homeless. Between two million and three million people are homeless at some point during the course of a year. The fastest growing segment of homeless people is families with children. Houghton estimates that nearly 30 percent of the homeless are children. In New York City alone 24,000 people show up at the shelters every night regardless of the danger to their safety. Another 25,000 to 35,000 people remain in the streets.

As awful as these numbers are, they don't even begin to address the problem of insufficient, low-income housing in America. The core of the problem is too few housing units at affordable prices. Real wages are down in America, and many people are forced to double-up, to share a room or a small apartment with a friend or relatives.

Morita's impression is that Americans see the world of business as a game. America has been deeply involved in mergers and acquisitions, he notes, and has built conglomerates of unrelated cash cows to support unimaginative, weakening industries. Temporarily cash-rich companies have sought glamorous, image-building additions to their corporate structure in order to dress up their annual reports, rather than promoting internal growth through retooling and reinvesting in product development. America buys and trades businesses, hoping to earn a profit on the spread. But sadly, these activities contribute nothing to society, nothing to the world. They build nothing for the future.

Morita says that America has forgotten this point. Instead of using money for its real purpose—to create jobs, new industries and new products—Americans use it to make individual people wealthy. The price the United States pays is the loss of its manufacturing base. America is being driven onto an industrial lee shore and is being made to make the most of a service economy. Instead of a nation of brawny steelworkers making an income sufficient to support their families, America is fast becoming a land where hamburger flippers and clerks make up the majority of the work force, where two wage-earners are required to put bread on the table, and where children must learn to live with a latchkey instead of a parent. As a result, "It is unlikely that the United States will ever again be able to provide for even its own most basic needs," Morita says.

It's not that these facts are unknown in America—that is not the problem. On the contrary, America swears by them. Morita is right, greed has become king in America. When John Welch, the Chairman of the Board at General Electric, announced in November 1989 that G.E. would buy back 10 billion dollars worth of its own stock over the next five years, the Wall Street analysts were deliriously happy. This was the largest stock buyback announcement in U.S. business history. In the next eight months, G.E. stock rose from $55 to $74, an increase of almost 35 percent. Can you guess what this did to the personal wealth of John Welch? The following chart will show you not only the enormous 1989 salaries and current bonuses, but also the deferred bonuses and the improvement in the personal wealth of G.E.'s top three managers.[9]

COMPENSATION FOR 1989
GENERAL ELECTRIC'S TOP THREE OFFICERS

NAME	Cash Compensation[10]	Deferred Bonuses[11]	Stock Gain[12]
John F. Welch, Jr.	$2,648,700	$4,116,100	$9,171,110
Lawrence Bossidy	$1,782,200	$2,741,800	$4,429,280
Edward Hood, Jr.	$1,437,900	$2,289,900	$3,811,932

Welch justifies General Electric's buying back its own stock as a better way of generating value for shareholders than taking a "wild swing" on an acquisition, or investing in new technology. This is a new concept in business management and investing and one that should be included in college textbooks. For if this is truly the direction that America wants to take, and truly the attitude that successful managers need to develop, then the managers of the future should learn as early as possible how best to exploit the nation for their personal gain.

Welch's actions exemplify the way the meaning of the word "investor" has changed. Instead of taking a long-term interest in a company's future prospects by creating new markets with new products, an investor is now anybody in the stock market for short-term profit potentials. The idea is quick turnover: Get in and get out as fast as you can, and make money on the spread. What happened? Did somebody redefine the English language while we weren't looking? In the past, those people have always been scorned as speculators and gamblers. They were not applauded in the business press.

Instead of finding a way to get tough and compete with the Japanese in television production, G.E. abandoned the market. They fled from VCRs, and gave up on radios. They sold off all of their small home appliance businesses. They looked at superconductors and trembled. As a result, General Electric has signed its own death warrant. It will begin to decay and wither in a garden of safe products with limited life spans.

Unfortunately, Welch is not alone. Lazy managers without any guts are the rule these days. John Akers of IBM is in the same boat. How can the world's leader in computers have missed the laptop market? What progress has been made in developing color screens for laptops? Can it really be true that not one American company stuck with U.S. LCD technology, and that now laptop computer screens can only be bought from Japan? It will be no surprise to see who introduces the first color screens in this market. You can bet good money that it won't be IBM or any other American company.

IBM still thinks of itself as an unassailable giant alone in the world. It refuses to believe that it is vulnerable, that the Japanese have the power to destroy competitors. It refuses to cooperate with other American computer manufacturers on setting a unified American standard for a disk operating system which would help narrow the struggle against Japanese competition. Even its recent alliances with Apple, Intel, Thinking Machines, Siemens and Motorola are self-serving schemes to protect narrow marketing plans at the expense of meeting the long-term, more serious, challenge from Japan. Yet, IBM saw the need to buy back billions of dollars of its own stock. It could find nothing of interest that needed further research and development, nor any new products or markets in which to invest the money. Somebody obviously thought it more important to line his own pockets—and to hell with the company's future.

Akers' 1990 compensation from salary, stock options and restricted stock grants amounted to 7.4 million dollars.[13]

Roger Smith, who retired in July 1990 as Chairman of the Board of General Motors, also belongs in this club of deep-pocketed managers without any vision. Only 15 years ago G.M. had a 50 percent share of the United States automobile market. Today, its share has shrunk to one third, and thousands of American workers have been turned out into the streets. Robert Stempel, General Motors' new Chairman of the Board, comes from the same mold. He had the nerve, in January 1992, to announce the coming layoffs of 74,000 more employees, and the expected loss of over four billion dollars on operations. This is the biggest one year loss in the history of American business. Yet he saw the wisdom in taking 1.6 million dollars in compensation in 1991. And that does not include perquisites such as free cars and first class corporate jet air travel for him and his wife, or stock options.

Lee Iaccoca at Chrysler has obviously gotten tired after all the work he did getting the U.S. government to save his company from its bankruptcy. He has shown himself to be just another fat cat with a yen for one more buck. He took 4.5 million dollars in compensation in 1991, not counting the extras. Yet, his company is on the verge of bankruptcy again. Why does Chrysler need to buy automobiles from Japan? How does that help Chrysler in the long run, or the U.S. economy?

Hewlett-Packard, Ford Motor Company, Digital Equipment, Apple Computer. The list goes on and on. Even small software companies such as Lotus Development are buying back their shares. When they do this, they advertise themselves as visionless companies with no plans or hopes for the future.

The companies' rationale is that they are leaders in the markets they have chosen to pursue and are investing important resources in those areas. In fact, they are leaders in markets that the Japanese have not yet targeted. These companies are looking for a niche where they will be safe from the winds of competition. What they fail to realize is that the Japanese are not niche marketers. Japan will take a whole market if it decides to invade that market. A niche has a way of disappearing in a big wind.

Superconductors, for example, are about to revolutionize world transportation. Anybody who cannot see the coming market for ultra fast ships without propellers, trains that don't need tracks, and airplanes that fly without jet engines, not to mention automobiles that will not need gasoline, has no concept of the powerful Japanese vision. These things will happen, and it will be the Japanese who will market them. We are not talking about the year 2092, but rather the next 20 years.

The Honda Motor Company budgets five percent of its anticipated sales every year for research. Nippon Electric (NEC) invests seven percent of sales in research. These figures are reached regardless of profit levels in any year. Almost no U.S. company reaches these levels of investment in its own future. Is it any wonder that Japanese companies are now leading in U.S. patent approvals granted?

The Japanese have spent billions of dollars over the past few decades in rebuilding their industrial base. They have invested hundreds of millions more dollars in buying influence in the United States, influence that has opened American markets to Japanese products under terms that gave Japan an incredible competitive advantage.

Japan's government policies have forced the Japanese people into one of the highest personal savings rate on earth. The fastest capital-formation machine known to man has been the result of these policies. By restricting the availability of imported merchandise in Japan, the government has limited consumer goods selection to those items made at home. Until recently, that selection has been much narrower than in other world markets. The result is that the Japanese people have saved their money rather than spend it on excessively high-priced imported merchandise or because what they wanted wasn't available. Japan has made only modest attempts in the past year or two to open its markets to allow foreign competition. Instead, it is actively pursuing plans to further pummel into submission American industries such as aerospace, medical equipment, large computers and even banking and investment brokerage services.

Another example of America's decline is seen in management's attitudes towards organization. Years ago, in 1977, Sears, Roebuck's then-Chairman of the Board, Arthur Wood, gave an address to a gathering of his New York executives. His message was that he saw the Chairman's role as "conservator of Sears assets." His job was to do nothing that would harm Sears long-term financial position. Wood sounded just like Sewell Avery of

Montgomery Ward in the 1940s when that company began its long decline. Yet, Sears' CEO couldn't stop there and be content to watch Sears falter; he had to spur its demise. Wood reported that he had hired McKinsey and Associates, management consultants, and, at their suggestion, was adding a new layer of management between the frontline troops and himself. He also created an Office of the Chairman which turned a formerly effective chief executive officer into an office of bureaucrats. These changes were necessary to implement his policy of doing nothing and taking no risks.

In the meantime, of course, the growth of K mart and Wal-mart proceeded apace. Now, both of these chains' sales exceed those of Sears. Sears: The world's largest merchant? Used to be. Look at all the specialty stores in existence today, and the array of mail order catalogs. And Sears' pathetic answer is Brand Central and "everyday low prices." It has never recovered from Wood's dispersion of decision making power.

In 1964, just before the Age of Aquarius and the beginning of hippiedom in American management style, Sears, Roebuck's strength was its decentralized management. Every store manager and every buyer was a little king unto himself. Each could react on his own authority to market changes, and do so quickly. Obviously, a manager was held accountable for his decisions, but the system worked. Sears was the leader. But as the starry-eyed clan came to power and began centralizing decision making procedures in the haze of Chicago headquarters, management contact with the customer was lost. Reaction time to market changes slowed. Sears became a third-rate merchant on its way out, hard on the heels of Robert Hall and Grants.

Professor Richard Rosecrance of the University of California at Los Angeles, author of *America's Economic Resurgence: A Bold New Strategy*, has dug up some pertinent data on this subject. "At General Motors, 77.5% of the work force is white collared and salaried."[14] Rosecrance goes on to relate the similarity of other companies' heavy management-to-worker ratios. It's not only Sears. At Mobil Oil it is 61.5% white collar. At General Electric the figure is 60%. At DuPont, 57.1%. "The ratio in typical corporations in Japan is about one-sixth of the American figure."[15]

Rosecrance also wrote that, "If the United States is to arrest its decline, two developments need to occur in the near future: first, American business will need to increase the ratio of operators to managerial staff, giving management a much wider purview; second, workers will increasingly come to fulfill a management function. In the more distant future, the distinction between white and blue collars may disappear."[16]

Occasionally, there is news of an American company that seems to have learned its lesson and is beginning to fight back. Motorola is such a company. Some years ago, it took its licking and got driven out of the television and radio business. But Motorola managed to survive by getting into a lean management structure and by devoting about eight percent of its sales to research. Not surprisingly, this policy has made it the major contender in the mobile telephone and pager business. Motorola is now number one in Japan, beating NEC, Casio and Matsushita. It can be done.

One of the major reasons why Morita believes that the United States is in decline is because of the American government's attitude toward money. The Japanese do not care for a floating exchange system, and have been dissatisfied with the world monetary system since the abandonment of fixed rates at Bretton Woods. Morita's belief is that money should not be the subject of speculation. It should be tied to a solid, substantial unit of real value, such as gold.[17] The purpose of money is not to make speculators and banks rich. Its purpose is to smooth the path for production activities. Of course, Japan's concern about the value of money arises in part from the depth of its investment in the United States.

The flow of capital from Japan to the United States exceeded 120 billion dollars a year from 1986 through 1988 and was over 80 billion dollars in 1989 and 1990 (est.).[18] "In the U.S....Japanese banks held a reputed 20%-plus of the banking system's assets..."[19] "Real estate brokers can tell you that Japan invested $15 billion in Hawaiian real estate between 1985 and 1990."[20] It really galls the Japanese to see the value of their investment being dissipated by the relative U.S. inflation when they have done such a good job at home of controlling prices.

To the Japanese the fault of America's decline lies with the United States. They do not feel that they should be blamed for doing what the U.S. should have been doing over the past thirty years. They mention it in every round of trade negotiations. They have never forced anybody to buy their products. Can they be blamed, they ask, if they make the best products on the market, and sell them at reasonable prices? Is it their fault that Americans recognize quality and value and buy Japanese? Did the Japanese force their American competitors out of business, or did U.S. manufacturers just roll over and quit when the competition got tough?

This argument is only partially fair. In a later chapter we will talk about dumping and other Japanese tactics for gaining market share. These are points that cannot be ignored.

A real problem with the American economy needs to be looked at strategically. If American investors are content to live by shuffling money around foreign exchange counters and junk bond markets, which only serve cannabalistic leveraged buyout schemes, and by spending their profits on raiding other companies, rather than in developing new products and new markets, then they will have to learn to live with the consequences. Those consequences are a permanent dependence on imported manufactured goods and a declining standard of living. If the American people are willing to gamble on the good sense of bank managers to invest their savings in the stock market, then they deserve whatever result befalls them. These decisions have been made in the past without the participation of the American people, and they are far too important to be left any longer up to an "investor class." Congress must get involved in deciding what America will do with its national wealth, what goals will be pursued, and which investment schemes will be outlawed. These decisions are much too important to be left to executive branch agencies.

If ever a national debate was needed on the direction of America, it is now. If the next ten years are allowed to develop economically along the same lines as the past decade, the prospect is a geometric growth in the numbers of homeless and underprivileged people in this country. The lives of minority groups, long oppressed by limited job opportunities, will become intolerable. Even WASPs are beginning to feel the pinch of layoffs, early retirements and narrowed fields of opportunity available to their children. It has become an accepted condition of life that the next generation may never own its own homes without significant parental contributions.

Morita, in his book, tells of making a speech in Chicago that he titled "Ten Minutes Versus Ten Years." He told the group that the Japanese typically plan their business strategies ten years in advance. When he asked an American money trader if he planned even a week ahead, the reply was, "No, maybe ten minutes." "At that rate," Morita told his Chicago audience, "you will never be able to compete with us."

While Morita's example of an American arbitrageur may not have been the fairest comparison, his point that money is capital is worth considering. America is a capitalistic society, although it seems to have degenerated into something less noble today. It is only when its citizens forget that money is capital, that capital's primary purpose is to be channeled back into new plant and equipment, that they get a terrible savings and loan debacle. Unshackling the S & Ls from their strict investment guidelines back in 1980 and 1982 was an anti-capitalist gesture. It would not have been a more effective blow against our system if Marx and Lenin themselves had designed the strategy.

The same reckless attitudes about money and investing are also plaguing the banking industry. L. William Seidman, Chairman of the Federal Deposit Insurance Corporation, in testimony before the House Banking Committee on April 11, 1991, said that growing commercial bank losses were the result of deregulated real estate lending practices, and he urged Congress to reinstate tougher rules. Commercial banks, he said, have been lending against undeveloped land, making unusually long term loans, lending on speculative commercial building projects, requiring less owner equity and operating on a narrower spread than normal between interest paid on deposits and interest earned on loans. "It's time for insured institutions to return to old-fashioned standards [pre-1974] of safe-and-sound banking," urged Seidman. This stance put him at odds with the Treasury Department's plan to overhaul the nation's banks, and it put finish to his career at the FDIC.

But all is not entirely lost. There are always a few examples that American vision may still be alive. IBM, to its credit, in May 1990, stepped in to help save the Perkin-Elmer optical lithography division from being bought up by the Japanese. It orchestrated the purchase by a California company, the Silicon

Valley Group. This Perkin-Elmer division makes the machines needed to manufacture the most-advanced silicon chips. If Nikon had been allowed to purchase the company, the United States would have lost this important semiconductor manufacturing technology and might never have been able to catch up with Japan.

Furthermore, the choice of Dr. William J. Spencer to replace the late Robert N. Noyce as head of Sematech, the government and industry chip-making consortium, is turning out to be a good choice. Dr. Spencer, a physicist, had been the Chief Technical Officer at Xerox Corporation, and has led a variety of semiconductor research programs. It had looked for a while as if this association of 14 American semiconductor manufacturers might drown in a sea of bickering. That would have been unfortunate. Sematech recently released industry data showing that for each one percent loss in semiconductor market share, 5,470 industry jobs are lost and the United States government loses 200 million dollars in tax revenue. The figures were compiled by the Semiconductor Industry Association.

And much like the Japanese HSST group, in a recent billion-dollar attempt to revolutionize the automobile industry, a number of American utility companies, Detroit's Big Three, and the U.S. Department of Energy have joined to form the Advanced Battery Consortium. The Consortium intends to develop the ideal battery—a battery that would help replace the combustion engine, the inefficient gas guzzler that powers today's automobile. The companies expect to extend battery life to ten years by the year 2000, simultaneously cutting costs and extending the battery's range.

However, in the overall story of America, Perkin-Elmer and the Advanced Battery Consortium are exceptions. The theme being played out in America today is one of short-term money making. Stocks are owned and managed primarily by large institutions, and these investment companies' sole responsibility is to maximize profits by trading the shares. They are not investors: They are traders. And they have some nerve expecting the government to grant them capital gains tax exemptions.

In years past, America was fortunate to have consortiums of investors to build railroads and the oil industry. They opened mines, cleared land and built steel and textile mills. They invested in shoe factories that planned to make shoes rather than to acquire ice cream stands. These investments were for the long-term, for development of new products and industries.

Today, the name of the game is quick profits, not building a business or supporting an industry. Massive stock trades take place instantaneously on computer-generated buy and sell recommendations that are based on market trends. The price and volume movements can be so volatile that individual investors fearing a heavy loss are often driven out of the market. Long-term investments have become financially impossible.

If the vaunted American service economy is to be built on financial services, then Americans are worshipping a chimera. When investors do not leave their money in long-term projects, such as they do with the many ten year projects in Japan, then the American economy loses substance. Japan spent a fortune and many years developing practical uses for semiconductors while Americans were content to smile at the novelty of their invention. The Japanese are doing the same thing with superconductors and the aerospace business. America must return to a real production dominated economy or face a bleak future of growing poverty.

Sadly, America sees itself entering a futuristic society of information and intelligence processing, insurance and financial services. It doesn't understand that this new society will produce nothing of material value. The United States, and most of Europe for that matter, has forgotten that the nature of capitalism is production. The essence of business is adding value to something and making it more than it was before. It seems unutterably strange that Americans should need the Japanese to remind them of this principle of capitalism.

Morita believes that Japan will continue to do well as long as it remembers to develop and manufacture products that have a tangible value. Any shift in national objectives toward the American concept of making a quick buck would spell the end of prosperity for Japan, just as it has for the United States and most European countries.

Not surprisingly, Morita recommends that America begin to emulate some of Japan's successful business strategies—sound advice if America really wants to revitalize its economy. For example, he advocates a change in American tax policy to penalize short-term stock market profits, and recommends a lower capital gains tax on investments held for many years.

In addition, he notes that of all the industrialized nations, the United States alone does not have a Department of Industry. There is no advocate in the government for business. He's right; had there been an organization equivalent to Japan's Ministry of International Trade and Industry, it is unlikely that the S & L scandal could have happened. There would have been voices shouting the alarm that the financial markets were becoming dangerously overcompetitive and that the new investment opportunities were too speculative. The American Department of Industry's job would be to project the consequences of major industry changes. Importantly, if ever the United States does create a similar agency, it must be a politically sensitive agency, in touch with the need for jobs. The Department of Commerce and the United States Trade Representative's office are charged with trade-related matters, not industrial development. Morita says that Ford and General Motors, for example, are supervised by the Department of Transportation, which is more interested in emissions control and highway safety, rather than in strategies for improving world market share and expanding employment opportunities.

What is needed is some powerful force at a national level that will fight for the reindustrialization of America and for the protection of its workers.

The American economy continues to deteriorate. Inflation is a never-ending problem and labor productivity grows too slowly. Moreover, interest rates are kept artificially high in order to attract enough foreign money to finance a huge national debt and a huge negative trade balance. Even the lower interest rates seen in 1992 are still higher than need be in a healthy economy. The Bush Administration began its term with high hopes of doing something about the debt and trade problems, but then became overwhelmed by the size of the Savings and Loan scandal and the growing bank problem, not to mention the enormous expense of the Persian Gulf War and the continued presence of U.S. troops in the Middle East and around the world.

The problem is that the Administration forgot the basic lessons taught in Economics 101: Service industries support capitalists. Manufacturing, using labor and tools to add value to materials, is capitalism. Service industries are not capitalists. They do not produce material wealth. Service industries cannot even exist if they do not have manufacturing industries to service. Disregarding this basic economic tenet means economic subservience to Japan forever.

Americans love a father-figure and Ronald Reagan was a wonderful one. Whatever he said, people believed, even though there is no reason to assume that he understood a fifth of what he said. To Reagan, they were all lines from a play, and he was the star. Trickle-down economics sounded wonderful. Laffer curves made great lines. Lower taxes made popular policy. People could buy whatever they wanted from all over the world with all the money in their pockets or by using their credit cards. Americans were living in Fantasyland.

How on earth does America expect to restore its economy? Do Americans believe that they can spend their way to prosperity? The Reagan Administration followed a program that can only be called consumerism. It was certainly not a capitalist program. It did nothing to encourage savings. There was no program to expand manufacturing or to improve America's export business, short of devaluing the dollar. Taxes were geared to serve speculators.

What happens when governments follow a policy of devaluing the dollar? It's like printing money: the effect is inflation. Big time investors know how to hedge their strategies to take advantage of inflation. They rarely get burned in an inflationary economy. The one who gets hurt is poor, works for a salary and tries to put aside a few dollars for a rainy day or retirement. The value of savings is destroyed by inflation. It is the cruelest tax known. Unlike a tax increase, inflation doesn't have to be voted on in the light of a free press. This year's government profligacy can be repaid next year with dollars that are worth less than the ones originally spent. The worker who needs to replace the family car finds that on a salary he or she can no longer afford to buy the same quality car. Americans have had to downsize or keep the old car longer. Clothes suddenly cost more. An average person can't afford to buy a house as his or her parents did years ago.

Morita suggests that the first step in controlling the national budget deficit should be an examination of gasoline prices in the United States. Regular unleaded gasoline is bargain priced at about $1.03 per gallon, and consumption is growing rapidly. Gasoline imports set record levels in 1989 and 1990 and filled over half of America's consumption needs. Demand slackened somewhat in the recession of 1991 and early in 1992, but the trend is still toward increasing reliance on imported oil. In the rest of the world gasoline sells for $2 to $4 per gallon, Morita notes. This is absurd self-pampering on America's part. He quotes the United States Department of Energy that a one-cent-per-gallon tax increase would yield one billion dollars in revenues each year, and he believes that would help significantly in reducing the national debt. Just imagine what good could be done if the tax were raised 25 cents, Morita suggests.

The fact is, that even with an additional 25 cents tax, the price of gasoline in the United States would still be cheaper than anywhere else in the world. But, Morita claims, politicians are afraid of not getting re-elected if they vote for additional taxes. Until the S & L scandal made him face reality, President Bush continued to swear that taxes would not be raised. "This is really creating credibility problems for America around the world," says Morita. Everybody else can see the solution to the twin deficit problems. Why can't the Americans?

The result of America's budget and trade deficits is a continual pressure in the world to divest dollars. The budget deficit in 1991 was over 350 billion dollars after reaching 220 billion dollars in 1990. The trade deficit annually exceeds 100 billion dollars. Only strong central bank intervention has kept the dollar from sliding even more than it has. But the price paid has been high interest rates. The Group of Seven central bankers and finance ministers at their meetings at the Plaza Hotel in New

York and at the Louvre agreed to support the dollar at levels that would assure the continuation of world trade. Without this support, the dollar would have gone into a free fall, creating both a recession and inflation in America. As it is, the U.S. economy has not been able to take advantage of this breathing space. Its structural flaws are too deep and its political torpor is too overpowering to avoid the inevitable. Consequently, the economy, in the fourth quarter of 1990, finally slipped into a recession that is turning out to be the longest since the Great Depression.

This is why relatively high interest rates will be a permanent factor of life in America if it is to keep attracting foreign investments which finance its huge national debt. During most of the 1980s Japan contributed significantly to moderating the rise in America's interest rates by heavily investing in U.S. Treasury bonds. However, in the 1990s, Japan now seems to feel that its money is better invested at home. And this has meant a dramatic reversal in the flow of Japanese funds: From an annual outflow of 100 billion dollars a year, it has shifted now to a 40 billion dollar a year inflow. Inflation is likely to continue to be a problem in the United States and further exacerbate its dependence on foreign investments.

Neither the Japanese nor the Europeans are likely to sit idly by and watch this deterioration of their investments in America. The American economy does not stand alone in the world. All economies are interdependent. Unless the United States takes some serious remedial action soon, a worldwide disaster is not just a worry, but a real possibility. In fact, the reported economic slowdowns in both Europe and Japan in the early months of 1992 may be the first signs of a world-wide recession. Much harder days may be in store for America if that happens.

In October 1987, soon after what became known as Black Monday, the Japanese Finance Ministry, according to Morita, asked all the Japanese institutional investors to support the American stock market prices. Because the action was swift and sufficient, stock losses were curtailed and the market collapse did not become a wipeout. A possible disastrous chain reaction of mindless selling was averted. Morita was demonstrating the importance of foreign capital, especially Japanese capital, to the U.S. economy.

If the current (1990s) withdrawal of Japanese funds from America had occurred during an economic expansion rather than during a recession, the U.S. might again have suffered a stock market crash. As it is, the recession has reduced the demand for capital in America, and the Japanese withdrawal is not being felt as strongly as it might otherwise.

Still, Morita brags that it was Japan that saved the American economy. And, implicitly, Japan can also do as much harm, if necessary. From 1985 through 1990 Japan spent a whopping 596.2 billion dollars in long-term foreign investments, mainly in the United States. From 1988 through 1990 Japan invested about 52 billion dollars each year in American factories, real estate and securities. However, in the first nine months of 1991, that figure dropped to 2.3 billion dollars. In 1988 the Japanese government bought 30.7 billion dollars in U.S. government securities. In 1992, Japan is a net seller of U.S. government securities.[21]

The Japanese government now has the financial strength to sustain Wall Street as well as the City of London, Morita crows. Japan has become a financial power, and like it or not, America has to recognize this fact. Americans have become, at least temporarily, dependent on foreign financing to keep afloat. But there is obviously no guarantee that Japan will always be available to refinance U.S. debt. What is happening in Japan is that its leaders now recognize the United States' dependence on them. This fact is bolstering their position in the world, especially in Asia where such things count for a lot. As a result, the Japanese people are being told that they should begin to behave in accordance with their new stature in the world and that their businessmen and diplomats should begin to assume more dominant roles in trade and diplomatic negotiations. They are being told that Japan is a world-class economic power, and that the Japanese ought to walk tall and act like leaders, a role that the Americans are rapidly abandoning.

CHAPTER FOUR
Prejudice

When the Japanese start yelling, "racist!", Americans need to remember that Japan is one of the most racially homogeneous countries in the industrialized world. In a population of 123 million people, the largest minority group is represented by less than 700,000 Koreans, most of them descendants of slave laborers brought to Japan before World War II. However, a few of these Korean families have been in Japan for generations, some with ancient names like Hata and Kamo which date back to the Yamato court in the fifth century. But even they have never been integrated into the larger Japanese community. No new immigrants are allowed.

A small number of Japanese aborigines, the Ainu, are mostly confined to the northern islands. These people are descendants of the original inhabitants of the Japanese islands. Both the Ainu and the Koreans are at the lowest economic levels in Japan. Neither group shares equally any of the opportunities in education, career advancement and housing or cultural life that are open to the Japanese.

So refined is the Japanese taste for discrimination that they have also banned over three million of their own people from any kind of meaningful participation in society. These people are called the *Burakumin*, similar to the caste that was known as the "Untouchables" in India. Ethnically Japanese, they are descendants of families employed as butchers, tanners, executioners and crematorium workers.

The Japanese seem especially turned off by dark-skinned peoples. A few years ago, they scandalized the world with their Sambo products: Restaurants, clothing and comic book characters. In 1986, Prime Minister Yasuhiro Nakasone declared that African-Americans and other minorities lower the I.Q. of America. The Filipino people are held in contempt and are considered a disorderly, unproductive race. Ishihara had some very unflattering things to say about Filipinos in his book. Recently, the Justice Minister, Seiroku Kajiyama, said that Japanese prostitutes ruin neighborhoods. Then, he added, "It's like in America when neighborhoods become mixed because blacks move in and whites are forced out."[1]

Even with the current worker shortage, the Japanese are reluctant to allow foreign laborers to settle in their racially pure homeland. A new law was passed recently to forbid foreign workers entry into Japan. The flow of thousands of illegal workers from Pakistan, Malaya and Bangladesh has now been stopped. Those who are still around are being deported as fast as they can be located. Under a new law, employers who hire these illegal immigrants face fines and up to three years in jail.

Unlike every other developed country from Canada to Switzerland, the Japanese have never subscribed to the notion that they have some obligation to share a portion of their prosperity with refugees. No one fleeing Vietnam or Hong Kong, and certainly no residents of the former Soviet Union, will find a welcome on the shores of Japan. "The Japanese government, along with other developed nations, 'said it would protect students after Tiananmen,' said Katsutoshi Fujimori, an attorney representing Chinese students in Japan. 'But it doesn't look like they plan to really honor that promise.'"[2]

Japan has often been criticized by human-rights advocates for its inhospitality toward political refugees. Many Japanese seem to fear that open immigration would disrupt the nation's social harmony.

The odd thing is that because skilled workers and managers are becoming so scarce in Japan (the unemployment rate hovers around one percent) Japanese corporations are behaving in very un-Japanese ways. Executive recruiters are hired to search for managers who are willing to bolt from their current employers. Working hours are being reduced and wages raised to attract and keep employees. Extended vacation time and other perquisites are being offered. Some companies, such as Canon, have found it necessary to move production offshore in spite of their desire to remain in Japan. For example, by late 1992 all of Canon's compact-camera production will move to China, Taiwan and Malaysia. This represents over four million cameras per year, and it is happening because enough labor cannot be found at home to get the job done. Still, immigrants need not apply.

Ishihara reports that he was shocked by the hostile attitudes among American Congresspeople toward Toshiba for its selling restricted, electronically controlled, precision machine tools to the then-Soviet Union. Rather than seek a legitimate political reason for this angry reaction, Ishihara chose to accept the explanation given by some of his old friends in both the Senate and the House of Representatives. They claimed the harsh resolution censuring Toshiba stemmed from racial prejudice.

It is certainly possible that Ishihara found a few American politicians who were willing to accept his charge of prejudice. Yet he never names any names. Moreover, the logic of his argument is skewed.

At first, Ishihara claims, American Congresspeople denied their reaction reflected any racial prejudice against the Japanese. They told him that there might be some lingering animosity among older Americans who had fought in the Pacific War. But, they themselves were not racist.

Ishihara took exception to that claim. He upbraided them for thinking that modern civilization was created and developed by Euro-American cultures. "Westerners, subconsciously at least, take great pride in having created the modern age."[3] This is a leap in logic that is extremely difficult for most Westerners to follow. How Ishihara jumps from a nebulous general prejudice to a Western theory of civilization baffles the mind.

Then, in a flight of fantasy that carries his argument into the realm of absurdity, Ishihara says that he told his congressional friends that though it may be true that the modern era is a product of the white race, the Western peoples have become too smug about it. In the Middle Ages, he reminds us, Asiatic races, such as Genghis Khan and his Mongolian armies, raided the European continent destroying towns and villages, looting and raping. With them they brought massive changes which were adapted into European lifestyles. People began to cut their hair short and shaved their eyebrows in imitation of the Mongol hordes. They began to walk with their knees apart in a menacing manner. He thinks that Genghis Khan probably became some sort of cult figure and that white women regarded him as a hero. In the official translation, he stops short on this point and says simply, "Even women liked the new styles."

The fact is that this man was Japan's Minister of Transportation and was, as late as 1989, being considered as a possible prime minister. While the former Minister of Transportation has a strange way of expressing himself, it seems likely that what Ishihara means to say is that the East has had as much cultural influence on the world as the West. Nowhere is the Asiatic contribution to the world of art in dispute except in Ishihara's mind. Even Japan's prowess in industrial organization, planning and production is admired in the West, feared too, sometimes, but admired nonetheless.

Ishihara cited one other example of American racial prejudice. During a trip to the United States in April 1987, he met with the United States Secretary of the Navy (In the official translation, "a senior U.S. Navy officer") to discuss the maritime navigational program known as the Amber System. Amber is the color of caution, and the system is named for just that concept. The way it works is that ordinary merchant vessels, tankers and container ships are equipped with sonar which can detect underwater objects. Most fixed objects, like reefs and other natural hazards, are already charted, but the merit of this system is that it can also detect submarines.

While the Amber System cannot tell the difference between Russian and American submarines, it can often detect a submarine's presence and then relay that information to the U.S. Navy. The Navy, of course, knows where its own submarines are located, and so, by elimination, can deduce the location of the Russian submarines.

Ishihara says that he suggested to the United States Secretary of the Navy that all Japanese commercial vessels be equipped with the Amber System. Japanese seamen, he reported, are reliable and cover all the seas regularly. Japanese vessels could gather this important data from all the major trade routes and pass it along to the Pentagon for U.S. analysis.

To Ishihara's surprise, the Americans told him that the Amber System and U.S. intelligence needs were none of Japan's business. He asked how, with a limited number of U.S. ships, the Americans could deny a need for help. To his shock, he was told that such a critical matter could not be left to Japan. Then Ishihara asked if it would be acceptable to involve the British and the Germans, and was told that it would be. Ishihara made no reference to the North Atlantic Treaty Organization, or to the 45 years of Cold War threat to those countries, or to the Western world's perceived need for collective defense planning. Nor did he mention, when it was helpful to his cause to ignore the subject, Japan's limited participation in its own defense during those same years. Without any historical perspective, Ishihara simply chooses a convenient example of Japan's being told to mind its own business, and calls it racial prejudice.

Ishihara slyly avoids mentioning that Japan would, through the Amber System, acquire knowledge of all the major submarine patrolling stations, both ex-Soviet and American, even if it could not readily distinguish between the two. Japan would then also have the option of passing the data on to whomever it chose. America must not forget that Japan has already sold restricted semiconductors and machine tools to the Soviet Union and parts for the F-14 fighters to Iran and threatened to do it again.

Ishihara says that in American minds, even the ex-Soviets are more trustworthy than the Japanese. American racial prejudice toward Japan is an ingrained character trait, and the Japanese ought to be wary and keep this fact in mind when dealing with the United States. If this were only one man's invective, America could ignore him and get on with Japanese-American relations. Unfortunately, Ishihara's attitude appears to reflect widespread feelings.

During World War II, America and the United Kingdom bombed civilian targets in Germany, but only in Japan did America use the atomic bomb. This fact is the most commonly expressed summary of Japan's World War II experience. On the anniversaries of the destruction of Hiroshima and Nagasaki, the Japanese newspapers recount the terrible loss. They try to explain to their readers why it happened, and they can never come up with a satisfactory answer. Why Japan and not Germany?

Few nations in the world, if any, have suffered such an immediate devastating loss of life. Yet the most unfortunate aspect of these bombings is not the immediate loss of tens of thousands of lives, but rather the long-term psychological damage done to tens of millions of living Japanese. It simply is not acceptable to them that the bombs were not ready in time to use against Germany. The only thing that makes any sense to the Japanese is that they were the victims of a malevolent racial prejudice. These bombings were too awesome to have been matters of chance timing. There had to be something more involved. Racial prejudice is the only explanation they can accept.

Many Japanese believe that one of their characteristic faults is a chronic inability to say "no"—particularly to international trading partners. This concern is reflected by the wistful title of Ishihara's book. *The Japan That Can Say No* is a vision of a nation that, in the authors' eyes, has yet to develop its full potential for aggression. But perhaps they are over-modest.

At any rate, throughout the country, businessmen and diplomats are being encouraged to speak out more frankly. This trend is reflected in part by the series of shocking comments on African-Americans made in recent years by several prominent Japanese figures.

A fundamental behavioral change among the Japanese is necessary, according to Ishihara (and Morita), to avoid a repetition of what has, in Japan, come to be known as "The Towers Incident." Many Japanese wrongfully ascribe the incident to an inexplicably vicious act of disrespect by the American government—rather than to simple error on the part of the U.S. Naval Commander.

The Towers Incident occurred on November 9, 1988, and was extensively reported on in the Japanese media but almost ignored in the United States. The U.S.S. Towers (DDG 9) a guided missile destroyer sailing just outside Yokosuka Harbor and about to approach Tokyo Bay, fired a five-inch unarmed shell in a target practice exercise. This caliber shell weighs 70 pounds and can travel a distance of 14 miles, so it is potentially dangerous even without an explosive charge. The shell in question landed in the water very close to the MSA Uraga, a Japanese Coast Guard patrol boat. The Japanese were incensed. And when their Ministry of Foreign Affairs tried to cover up the affair, they became, undoubtedly, even angrier. In the naval inquiry which followed, the U.S. ship's captain was relieved of his command. An official U.S. government apology was extended to the Japanese people.

Obviously, that was an unacceptable incident; it should not have happened. Yet, it is also important to remember that where one has guns and other implements of war, one will have accidents. The bigger the guns, the bigger the accidents. The United States Navy has been having a series of tough luck incidents over the past several years that have cost the lives of hundreds of sailors, not to mention the loss of many millions of dollars in equipment damage. If the Navy is to continue patrolling Japanese waters, other incidents could occur. If the Japanese prefer that this duty be left to them, all they should do is speak up. But it is demagoguery to claim discrimination and prejudice every time an accident occurs.

"The U.S. military probably believes such actions are permissible, because they are defending Japan under the Japan-

U.S. Security Treaty. But I have to think that the watchdog, in this instance, had become a mad dog."[4]

Ishihara deliberately uses the term "mad dogs" when referring to the Americans, because he remembers that Etsusaburo Shiina, Deputy President of the Japanese Liberal Democratic Party, used this term when he was Foreign Minister. This Towers Incident, he says, is one concrete case when it would have been in Japan's best interest to tell America "No, this conduct is unacceptable." One must learn to say no when he or she means no. "Failure to stand up to the Americans only stimulates their racial prejudices."

The Japanese people, Ishihara claims, should understand that now it is they who protect the United States, not the other way around. "This is a new era in Japanese-American relations. The Americans, at least in the more informed circles, seem quicker to grasp this fact than do our own Japanese citizens. It's time for Japan to walk proudly as a world leader."[5]

These sentiments are not uncommon for any nation that has had the economic success that Japan has had over the past 40 years. But it is easy for Japan to forget that the Unites States has been spending about six percent of its gross national product on defense needs every year since World War II to protect the free world from what everybody had thought were the dangers of Communism. The Japanese had to be cajoled into spending a mere one percent of their gross national product on defense. The difference in these drains upon their respective economies has been significant.

CHAPTER FIVE

Trade Discrimination

At every practical level where trade discrimination can be measured, the United States, Canada and Europe emerge as free trade activists in comparison with the Japanese. Owen Bieber, president of the United Auto Workers, made some insightful observations in an article in the May 13, 1990 issue of *The New York Times*. He was reporting on Japanese investment in the United States, though the same case can be made as well for Japanese investments in Europe. Bieber claims that the competition Japan offers its domestic rivals is based on unfair advantages and manufacturing methods.

Namely, "Japanese auto companies are not using their transplanted capacity to replace automobiles imported from Japan, but to expand their total share of the American market..."

Thus, "although the new transplant facilities are highly efficient, much of their cost advantage...results from tax deals, training grants and other incentives from states and localities. It also results from lower fixed health-care and pension costs associated with a new and generally younger workforce."[1] In other words, on a level playing field where U.S. and Japanese manufacturers compete under the same conditions, the U.S. can do as well as anybody.

For example, in an effort to attract the Nissan automobile assembly plant to Smyrna, the state of Tennessee offered the

Japanese company "$20 million in tax incentives, training programs and infrastructure improvements."[2]

Another case involves the Mitsubishi-owned company, Diamond-Star and its automobile factory in Bloomington, Illinois. William Holstein, author of *The Japanese Power Game*, wrote, "Illinois subsidized all of this (the plant and its parts suppliers) by assembling a package of incentives for Diamond-Star of as much as 177 million dollars, which affected local, state and federal governments. Such incentives as tax abatements, training, road improvements, water and sewage improvements, and reduction in federal import duties were put in place." He concludes that, "In effect, the U.S. government has one set of rules that apply to American companies in America, and another set that applies to Japanese companies in America."[3]

Because the United States does not have any foreign content legislation, as does Europe, only 38 percent of the parts that the Japanese assemble in North America are manufactured locally. But even that figure is misleading, because it does not describe the methodical discrimination against American-owned parts suppliers. According to the University of Michigan's Office for the Study of Automotive Transportation, 90 percent of the parts that go into cars manufactured by the Japanese come from Japan or from Japanese-owned suppliers with factories in the United States.[4]

In 1990, the Big Three auto companies produced only 62 percent of cars sold in the United States. Imports captured 26 percent of the sales and Japanese transplants (Japanese-owned factories in the U.S.) another 12 percent. In theory, therefore, Japanese investment is helping to sustain the domestic U.S. auto industry, simply substituting for American owners, but in practice this is only partly true. The transplant factories rely heavily on Japanese machine tools and production technology. Despite claims to the contrary, only about half of the total value of the transplant cars is produced in the U.S. Some parts are directly imported. Many others come from new Japanese plants that in turn import components from Japan.[5]

These studies suggest that American parts manufacturers are being locked out of their own market because they are not members of a Japanese *keiretsu*, an association of Japanese firms that band together to support each other's businesses. In part, this happens because American managers are seldom in charge of Japanese plants. They usually have only nominal control. A Japanese manager is lurking somewhere in the background to oversee and overrule the American's decisions. This is especially true in a matter as important as selecting a parts supplier. The meaning behind this policy of Japanese control is that, in reality, Japan has only transferred low-skilled jobs to the United States. Engineering and other high-skilled, decision-making jobs are reserved for workers in Japan.

Japan is willing to buy Alaskan crude oil because Alaska's proximity reduces ocean freight charges. Japan buys raw cotton from the southern states and unprocessed logs from the north-western states. It will accept Pacific salmon in bulk, or Atlantic cod transferred to Japanese ships. When Japan brings its operations to U.S. shores it will allow American labor to do rough assembly work, but few of the managerial functions.

Although American ideas and inventions are welcome, especially since Japan doesn't have to pay for them, it doesn't want American parts. In short, the Japanese are happiest when they can treat the United States and Europe as if they were underdeveloped countries whose sole purpose is to supply raw materials for the great Japanese manufacturing plants.

Ishihara believes that the future will bring changes: "It is being born now in the East." He suggests that Japan will be the leader of this new era and that the United States should begin to prepare its people for these changes. Otherwise, the workers of America will not know their role in the future society. Ishihara neglected to add that his version of society will be directed by local Japanese managers.

In an interview with *The Wall Street Journal*, Professor Mordechai Kreinin of Michigan State University reported on the operations of 62 multinational corporations in Australia. Of these, 42 were owned by Western interests and 20 by the Japanese. In the Western-owned companies, the plants contained manufacturing equipment from all over the world. "By contrast, the overwhelming preponderance of the equipment used in the Japanese-owned factories came from Japan."[6]

Kreinin said in this same interview, "The Japanese are different. When an American or European company buys machinery to set up a plant, they take competitive bids. But the Japanese go directly to Japan."

Another telling factor in Japanese-American trade relations, where Japanese-style capitalism takes its toll on the United States' balance of payments, is the growing influence of local Japanese companies on over-all trade figures. Norman Glickman and Douglas Woodward reported in their book *The New Competitors* that Japanese-affiliated companies in the U.S. imported 71.1 billion dollars worth of goods in 1987 while exporting only 20.8 billion dollars of goods. The difference, about 50 billion dollars, was about the size of the U.S. trade deficit with Japan that year.

The reason the Japanese are so angry is difficult for most Westerners to understand. After all, their economy is thriving and they are exporting at record rates. Such an economic picture in any other country of the world would look marvelously promising. The chart below shows just how favorably the

Japanese economy compares to that of the United States. It is misleading only in the respect that a Japanese citizen, even with a higher per capita GNP, cannot buy as much with his net income as an American citizen. That's because the Japanese home market is protected from competition by imports. As a result, in terms of purchasing power, the Japanese are only about 80 percent as well off as Americans.

A COMPARISON OF THE FISCAL 1991 AMERICAN AND JAPANESE ECONOMIES

	U.S.	JAPAN
Population (est. in millions)	253.9	123.4
Gross Domestic Product (billions/$)	$5,674	$2,990
Inflation (in percent)	3.6%	2.4%
Gross Private Investment (%/GNP)	13.5%	25.5%
Savings (% Hsehold disp. inc.)	5.2%	14.3%
Per Capita GNP	$21,166	$24,237
Interest Rates (30 yr gov't bonds)	7.82%	5.87%

Sources: Organization for Economic Cooperation & Development, U.S. Dept. of Commerce, (Survey of Current Business), Dept. of Census, Bureau of Labor Statistics, Japan Economic Institute, International Monetary Fund

At the Japan Center for Economic Research in Tokyo, Hisao Kanamori, the chairman, confidently predicts that Japan's economy will grow at an average of five percent per year in the 1990s while the U.S. economy will grow at only a three percent rate. If this holds true, by the end of the century Japan's economy will be much closer in size to the United States. Kanamori's estimates are very conservative for Japan and extremely optimistic for the United States. Closer to the mark would be to project

Japan's GNP growth at 5.5 percent per year and 2.5 percent for the United States. The real danger, though, is that a prolonged recession in America is likely to narrow the differences between our countries even faster than has yet been predicted.

The key to Japan's economic growth can be found in its much higher rates of personal savings and corporate investment. Japanese corporations do not spend their profits on raiding other Japanese corporations. They invest in new plants and equipment and in more product research or market development.

What worries the Japanese most is that with America's growing foreign debt, a day may soon come when the United States will renege on its massive interest payments. Shunji Taoka, a writer and editor for an influential Japanese magazine, *Aera*, speculates in an interview with *The New York Times* that to get out from under its depressing burden of debt, the United States might do either or both of two things. One, print money irresponsibly, creating enormous inflation to pay off dear money loans with cheap money. Or, it might reinvade Japan and try to cancel its debts by force.[7]

This last speculation is usually only whispered in conversations with Japanese businessmen and politicians. However, it affects Japanese decision-making. On the one hand Japan sees trade opportunities with the United States, but on the other, it worries about growing American protectionist attitudes. The Japanese see themselves as the victims, and not the perpetrators, of trade discrimination.

Wataru Hiraizumi is a member of Japan's Liberal Democratic Party and has a seat in the National Diet (Parliament). He says, speaking of the Twentieth Century, "The big problem was not the Cold War, but the question of Germany, Japan and the U.S.... People don't realize how dangerous the U.S. can be."[8] Hiraizumi believes that the Americans' worst fault is that they think of themselves as superior beings. He refers to the United States as a nation of heterogeneous immigrants who have grown up with a history of individuality. This fact makes it impossible for Americans to cooperate with the rest of the world.

These views on the far side of the Pacific Ocean are balanced by ex-Commerce Secretary Robert Mosbacher on this side. He appears to have been the only member of the Bush Administration to be at all concerned about Japan's threat to America's economic security. Unfortunately, the political pressure in Washington, D.C. can be enormous, and Mosbacher was forced to tone down his criticisms. Still, he managed to get quoted as saying, "You can't be allies with somebody you think is getting to you."[9]

CHAPTER SIX

MICHI: The Path or The Journey

There is a concept at work in Japan that is only partially understood in the West. It exists in the United States and in Europe, but it is much more important and institutional in Japan. This concept is the total mental and physical concentration on a goal or on a way of doing something; it is called *michi*.

Certainly, Western corporations have marketing and business plans, and often follow these plans religiously. Goals are important; they are not alien to the West at all. But the Japanese have taken discipline and concentration to an extreme that is seldom found in the rest of the world.

The simple task of making tea in Japan has been elevated to a ceremony. It is called *Cha No Ya*, and millions of Japanese study it. The tea ceremonialists are awarded various colored belts, as in karate, indicating progress in proficiency. As far back as the 16th century Momoyama Period, tea master *Sen no Rikyu* had set the standards for the types of bowls to be used. The Ido bowls, resembling Korean peasant rice bowls, are best. The way the whisk is held is critical, as well as the number of strokes per minute. The tea must be beaten with a prescribed delicacy and the froth made to rise elegantly.

It's a mistake not to take the Japanese seriously. It's an error to ignore charges that sound frivolous or self-serving to Western ears. The Japanese sense of humor is not easily understood, and even when one appears to be pulling your leg, he is probably just having trouble saying what he means. The Japanese are always serious about what they say in negotiations; they take their ceremonies seriously. Humor does not relieve discipline in Japan as much as it does in the West. Yes, once in a while they will chuckle over something funny. But only rarely will the Japanese laugh at themselves—and then never in public.

One cannot understand modern Japan without comprehending the legacy of its past. *Seppuku*, or forced suicide as a disciplinary measure, was an integral part of their society. That kind of discipline tends to make people modest and self-effacing. The Japanese have learned to take comfort in the security of ritual.

In the West, society often points its finger at its own foibles and faults, and laughs at its shortcomings. In Japan that might well have resulted in a death sentence in years past, and this heritage has had its affect on modern Japan.

This cultural difference often causes misunderstanding between Japan and the West. Where Westerners are normally open and say what they want, the Japanese are more reserved and look for less personal gestures to express their needs. Granted, the Japanese feed their own xenophobic tendencies, but Westerners don't help matters either Japanese claims are simply dismissed without asking for further clarification. It's hard to get the Japanese to explain themselves, because it's bad manners for them to be too explicit. It is important to probe for details because, unless one does, the Japanese will not reveal the problem that is really bothering them.

The Japanese sometimes leave Westerners gasping in astonishment at the differences between them. For example, the emperor is not simply a man or an ordinary politician. For the past 2,000 years, the emperors have been seen as divine, descended from the sun goddess, Amaterasu. This is not a corollary to the Western royal rule by "divine right" where kings and queens held the throne with God's blessing. In Japan, the emperor is God.

It has only been since General Douglas MacArthur's personal decree in 1945 that the emperor has been officially relegated to human status. Today, with the growth in Japan's economic power bolstering confidence, a strong right-wing movement within the Liberal Democratic Party insisted that Emperor Akihito be reinstalled as a divinity following his coronation and made a "living god."

The majority of people in Japan, however, apparently have not yet caught up with their leaders on this question, and are not highly motivated to accept Akihito's divinity, according to Japanese newspaper polls. But like their pre-War Japanese parents, the younger generation seem ready to follow their leaders' decisions. They are proud of their country, but fearful lest they get into trouble with the rest of the world.

Yet the emperor's position in Japanese society is an issue of overwhelming importance, and it merits much more contemplation than it has received. In the absence of debate, the L.D.P. decided to go ahead with the private part of the coronation ceremony called the *daijosai*. The government reportedly spent 15 million dollars of public monies to finance this secret ritual. Emperor Akihito participated in a food-offering to the spirit of the founder of his lineage, Amaterasu Omikami. Afterward, he entered a private chamber occupied by two female Shinto priests and a ceremonial bed. It is unclear whether the experience was metaphysical or carnal, but the next day he emerged as a certified god.

Emperor Akihito's apotheosis could not have happened unless Japan felt secure enough to ignore Western criticism. As it turns out, few people in the West understand the significance of this action. The emperor's divinity crowns the success of the

Japanese industrial machine and sets the nation back on its path to ultimate glory—undisputed leadership and dominance of Asia. The divination is as if the nation had been awarded a black belt for achievement. It is the culmination of *michi*, and also the revitalization of the concept of *bushido*. The Japanese hierarchy will reemerge, the royal family (with all their titles) can now be resurrected, and the spirit of Japan restored.

What I have been describing is a nation of people who fear the West, and, at the same time, feel racially and culturally superior. They are hidebound by a closed society that forces them into an isolation that cannot permit Western-style outside relationships. When the Japanese get pointed in a certain direction, they cannot leave that path, *michi*. They are forced by their very natures to excel at details, such as tea whipping. The essence of being Japanese is to take any design, patent, copyright, invention or process, and make it better, faster, cheaper and smaller. The Japanese do not understand why they should be penalized by trade restraints for traits that they consider virtuous. Their path or journey through this world is made according to their own merits.

Unfortunately for North America, Europe and the rest of Asia, the path Morita and Ishihara have decided to take is the same self-sufficient, survivalist road that Prime Minister Hideki Tojo had followed in 1941. It is the same policy, perhaps with different nuances, expressed by Tojo's predecessor, Prince Fumimaro Konoye. It is the same argument that Yosuke Matsuoka used to divorce Japan from the League of Nations. The banner of Morita and Ishihara includes the charge that due to racial prejudice the United States is hindering Japan's destiny to become the primary power in Asia. With unfair trade barriers in the American market and by invading natural Japanese markets in China and Southeast Asia the United States is trying to slow Japan's natural growth.

Morita is worried about the growing anti-Japanese attitude in the United States. He doesn't understand America's two-faced policy of encouraging Japanese investment, yet remaining critical of the Japanese. Morita complains that the U.S. government has passed several harsh resolutions and trade barriers against Japan, while at the same time 37 different states have set up offices in Tokyo to promote Japanese investments. Congresspeople from these same states spend their time bashing Japan. It leaves him confused.

Morita claims American Congresspeople told him that if they were to say publicly that Japan is non-threatening, they would lose votes. They tell him that it is expedient to bash Japan, because it makes them look good. Morita says further that if a Congressperson smashes a Toshiba radio-cassette player with a hammer as the TV cameras are rolling, the Congressperson will gain national popularity and his or her votes will increase.

Individual states understand that if Japan invests in their local economies, the tax base is helped, employment rises and prosperity grows. Yet, the American people continue to be more and more critical of Japan. Morita finds this discouraging. One gets the impression that criticism of Japan ought to be discouraged by responsible American leaders, and that inconsiderate attitudes are interfering with Japan's progress on its path to world leadership.

The Japanese Federation of Economic Organizations, *Keidanren*, has established a Council for Investment in the United States. Its purpose is to make better investments, ones that have popular acceptance in the United States. The idea is to invest with public relations, as well as returns, in mind. If the politicians can't get votes by attacking Japan, then they will stop passing anti-Japanese trade laws.

Regardless of its publicly stated goal to become a member of the global community, Japan is bound by its history and by its culture. It's hard for the Japanese to socialize with Westerners. For example, in England the Japanese have started their own private golf clubs. A group of Japanese businessmen recently purchased the Old Thorns Golf and Country Club at Liphook, and another club is scheduled to be built in Denham, Buckinghamshire. They will play golf only among themselves, even if they have to buy their own country clubs.

Japan's investments in the United States also further its own nationalistic goals. If Japan must open up its domestic markets to American department stores, then it will elect to buy the stores that are allowed in Japan. Therefore, it should be no surprise to see the Japanese purchase Bloomingdales and Tiffany's, or to learn that Tiffany's now has expansion plans for its Tokyo store. Major real estate purchases are also typical investments. If rent must be paid, the Japanese prefer to pay it to Japanese landlords. Already, there is an effort underway to move more Japanese tenants into Rockefeller Center.

Sometimes it's easy to lose sight of *michi*, the path or the journey, in a discussion of Japanese investment and trade strategy. But if you look closely you begin to see a pattern. The Japanese build vertical organizations from raw materials to finished product, and they are all Japanese components. They want control of the products and markets that affect their lives and destiny. It isn't enough for Japan to simply contract for the purchase of American beef or Canadian logs.

Japan's desire for control can be seen in its purchase of thousands of acres of Midwestern farmland over the past few years. "Sixty Minutes" broke this story in the fall of 1990, televising Japanese cowboys herding cattle. The Japanese bought enormous cattle ranches and sent over their own cowboy managers. If they must import beef from the United States, then at least they will own the beef from the field to the table.

Automobile and other assembly operations being built by the Japanese in the United States have already been mentioned. Americans need the jobs, and that's no lie. As a result, many states and localities have ceded important tax advantages, made impressive real estate deals and offered grants to lure the Japanese plants to their regions. Still, parts for the assembly process come from other Japanese suppliers, and skilled labor is done by Japanese workers who are paid in yen at home. The Americans are left the less complicated chores. *Michi.*

Up until the time of Operation Desert Storm, the Japanese had become major foreign investors in United States Treasury Department bonds and in private equity offerings on Wall Street. The Japanese were so important, in fact, that they alone probably kept American long-term interest rates at about two points lower than they would have been without Japanese participation in the market. That began to change, though, with America's military involvement in the third world and the phenomenal growth of its budget deficit in 1991 to over 350 billion dollars. The American economy cannot tolerate for long the inflationary pressures that are building as a result of its military expenditures and profligate energy policy. The consequence of the Bush Administration spending policy is an increasing Japanese pressure on the United States to issue its debt in the more stable yen.

To fight inflation, the Federal Reserve Board has tried to keep interest rates high, but the recession that began in the fourth quarter of 1990 has played havoc with their plans. This dual scourge of inflation and high interest rates has interfered with a normal economic recovery. And now, in 1992, America finds itself, locked into stagflation yet again. As a sign of the times, there are many economists who see three and four percent inflation as no real problem. The Federal Reserve System, thankfully, has better sense, at least on those rare occasions when it is left to do its job without political pressure.

The United States' fragile economy has spurred the Japanese to begin looking for alternative investment opportunities. Frankly, there aren't that many investment opportunities in the world that can absorb all the yen available, but Japan has certainly begun to withhold some of its financial support from America. In 1991, Japan repatriated a net 36.6 billion dollars of its overseas investments.[1] When that starts to happen to a more significant degree, the United States may be forced into implementing some long-needed economic reform.

However, it is much more likely that the U.S. government will not be able to rouse itself to any serious action, and Americans will begin selling off the country at wholesale prices to keep themselves afloat for another year or two. Delay is the name of the game. Keep putting off the day of reckoning, because the choices the government would otherwise have to make are far too difficult. While the United States dithers over its current problems and has no defined future direction, the Japanese march in step toward common goals.

Over the long term it is probably the Japanese corporations, rather than its government, that will contribute most to Japan's building the "Pacific Era." Masahiro Yoshida, a managing director of Kubota Corporation, recently said that as his company begins its second century it has become necessary to develop a higher technology base for its business. Rice harvesters, tractors and water pipes are no longer sufficient to sustain the company's growth. As a result, Kubota has begun buying minority positions in such American corporations as Mips Computer Systems (microprocessors), Mycogen Corporation (microbial pesticides), and Stardent Computer Inc. (mini-super-computers).

The advantage to this policy is that Kubota's representatives are allowed to sit on the board of directors. In doing so, they become privy to American research directions and emerging technology. They learn how to direct their own home-based development programs, and are able to avoid the costly dead ends that the Americans may have turned down. Kubota is currently being sued by two former U.S. executives for an allegedly fraudulent transfer of Stardent's technology to a Kubota subsidiary.

Whether or not the technology is stolen, it does get transferred. Japanese policy, as typified by Kubota, is to take American technology and turn it into jobs at home. In their Tokyo plant, Kubota now builds graphics supercomputers designed by Stardent and minicomputers for Mips Computer Systems. *Michi.*

A different tactic is to buy an American subsidiary outright. Nippon Sanso KK of Japan, for example, tried to buy a semiconductor equipment subsidiary of Hercules, Inc. The susidiary, Semi-Gas Systems Inc., is so critical a part of America's national security that the Defense Department raised objections to the sale. They know where that technology would go. "The sale will leave us at the mercy of monopolistic control from Japan," said Rep. Douglas Walgren, (D–Pennsylvania), who chairs a House panel on America's competitiveness with Japan.[2] Thanks to this Congressman's help, the sale to Nippon Sanso KK was blocked, and Semi-Gas Systems was eventually sold to Matheson Gas Products, Inc. of Secaucus, NJ.

In Europe, it is the same story. Fujitsu Ltd., in late 1990, successfully negotiated the purchase of an 80 percent interest in Britain's largest computer maker, International Computers Ltd. When this deal was approved by the European Community, it made Takuma Yamamoto, CEO of Fujitsu, the kingpin of the world's second largest computer company after I.B.M.

NEC Corporation of Japan already has a 15 percent stake in the French computer manufacturer Cie. des Machines Bull that also owns Zenith Computer Systems, an American company. One Japanese investment, therefore, bought technology information in two Western companies. Unhappily, the purchase of a larger share of Machines Bull, and the loss of French control, also seems likely given Bull's lackluster profit performance and lack of marketing direction. Then, too, Olivetti of Italy appears to be another solid candidate for a Japanese takeover. Like many companies in the computer business, Olivetti has had trouble defining its role in the market. This flaw has left them with some huge losses. If both Machines Bull and Olivetti fall to the Japanese, it would just about foreclose Europe's ability to ever regain control of its own computer needs, not to mention control of its own defense requirements.

Another area that needs to be explored in greater detail, perhaps in a later book, is the Japanese ownership of, or participation in, Chinese, Korean, Singaporean, Taiwanese and other Southeast Asian corporations. One should be aware that while Japan's relations with other Asian governments, Korea, for example, may not always be cordial, business is always considered as something separate. Joint ventures that the U.S. Congress has approved with companies in those countries may not be wholly what they appear on the surface. Some technology has slipped past the U.S.' efforts to control it and has landed in unfriendly or uncooperative places such as Libya, Iraq, Iran, Pakistan, not to mention the former Soviet Union.

Some of Japan's more interesting European investments and joint ventures are reminiscent of the deals struck by the pre-War industrial alliances. In those days, extremely powerful corporate alliances, called *zaibatsu*, tried, often successfully, to dominate whole industries. Officially, *zaibatsu* are illegal today, but the post-War replacement, called *keiretsu*, operate in essentially the same way and often with the same power to control whole industries and markets. Seeing the Japanese revive these associations is causing more than a few quivers of fear among those Europeans who remember the war years.

One of these giant cartels has recently raised some serious worries in Europe. The Mitsubishi Group, one of the largest *keiretsu*, announced plans in March 1990 to work with Germany's Daimler-Benz AG on aerospace development projects. Daimler-Benz is Japan's largest foreign defense contractor. This move was made with complete disregard of Europe's natural skittishness over Japanese-German cooperation, especially in the field of high-tech armaments and aircraft engines.

Thirty days later, Mitsubishi Mining and Cement announced a merger with Mitsubishi Metal. These two groups had been forcibly separated after the war, and the reunion goes a long way toward re-establishing their former *zaibatsu*. The Japanese claim that these associations are essential to preserving Japanese competitiveness. Their entire just-in-time production system is based on this kind of cooperation between kindred companies. Iwao Nakatani, an economics professor at Osaka University, claims that without this organizational advantage, the "vitality of Japanese corporations will be seriously damaged."[3] Of course, he is right. Without the unfair advantage of *keiretsu* production and marketing, Japan could never have become so powerful.

In the United States and in Europe interlocking directorates, such as the Japanese *keiretsu*, are illegal, because they create unfair competition and do not operate in the public interest. Yet, Americans allow Japanese keiretsu to operate in the United States and to take advantage of American corporations, all in the name of free trade. It's as if the United States Congress has a death wish.

"Once you are part of an industrial group [*keiretsu*], you have no secrets. Your bank is the group's bank, and your company's financial details are available on request to senior group members," said one company president in Business Tokyo magazine.[4] Joining a *keiretsu* is like marriage, although it is a higher and more sacred alliance. This is one of the primary reasons why the American investor T. Boone Pickens, was kept off the board of Koito Manufacturing Co., though he owned 26 percent of the company. If he had been allowed on the board, Pickens could have learned too much about Koito's *keiretsu* partners which include the Toyota operations. This could never be allowed. Koito would have been expelled from the cartel. It would have destroyed Koito's business.

The thrust of all Japanese foreign investment, whether in the United States, Canada, Australia or Europe, whether sponsored by the government or by private business, is to advance Japan's agenda. *Michi*. The Japanese simply do not invest without clear objectives. Even the purchase of U.S. Treasury bonds is valued as much for the political influence as for the additional interest points that can be made.

Private Japanese companies have three solid reasons for spending money: To obtain access to scientific technology, to learn new systems and operations, to get a foothold in a new market or to expand their influence in already established markets. Japanese state capitalism is a reality. It is an enormously powerful competitor composed of interlocking government agencies, banks, industry groups, the military and politicians. Ordinary Japanese citizens are left out of this modern mega-*zaibatsu.* Today, the Japanese are led by twentieth century samurais in *savro* (Saville Row) business suits.

Regardless of Akio Morita's desire for a more effective public relations campaign, Americans, and other Western peoples, cannot continue to be duped. Public relations campaigns work best when they are based on truth. They begin to collapse when weighed down with lies. Americans like Japanese products, but do not like Japanese politics or business ethics. It angers Americans when U.S. ideas and designs provide production jobs for Japanese workers. Americans don't appreciate political pressure. They do not see a need to seek Japanese advice in relationships with other Asian countries. And they are suspicious of the exclusivity of Japanese social and business cliques. In short, the United States is a sovereign nation composed of individualists who have no intention of becoming obedient assemblers of the new Japanese Empire.

To Morita's credit, he urges the Japanese people working in America to become involved in local community service, and to stop being so shy about participation in local schools, charities and governments. At home in Japan Japanese men do not usually participate in local school affairs. It's the mother's duty to take care of educational matters. Morita suggests that Japanese men living in America learn to behave more like the natives.

While Morita doesn't expect his compatriots to get up on Sunday morning and go to church, he thinks it is unseemly for them to be seen with golf bags heading out to the country club at the same hour as their neighbors are leaving for Sunday School. He is very concerned about appearances.

The Sony chairman enjoys golfing in America, but he always does it with Americans. He takes his wife to the club, has dinner, and schmoozes with the boys. He notes that golf for most Japanese, even in America, is a business affair. The foursome is almost always Japanese, and after the game they have drinks by themselves all the while speaking Japanese. This only perpetuates the threatening image of foreign invaders, he says.

Morita wants the Japanese who live and work in America to become more socially active. It will help to reduce racial tensions. Japanese factories in America are usually located in rural areas where foreigners are more noticeable. Especially in these areas, it is vital that the Japanese do not form isolated communities. If the Japanese remain isolated from the local society, the local residents will vote for more Japan-bashing politicians.

Morita cites a few examples where Japanese companies have done things right. One company built a community center even before the plant became profitable. The town named the center after the company and gave the plant manager a *sayonara* party when he was reassigned.

Morita's goal is to reform American society to the point where Japan-bashing would lose votes for a politician. Currently, he believes that the Americans dislike the Japanese just for being Japanese. But if the Japanese working in America try to become a part of their local community, that attitude can be overcome, he says. Unfortunately, while it is certainly helpful for foreigners to seek a common ground with their neighbors, Morita has an incredibly naive point of view. It's hard to believe that a man of his stature, age and achievement could have learned so little about the world. Prejudice mostly has its basis in either economic or territorial disputes, not necessarily in ethnic distinctions. To eliminate Western prejudice against the Japanese, to the extent that it exists, Japan needs to address the economic issues that are causing it.

Morita also recognizes that our methods of communication are different in a cultural sense. The structures of the Japanese and English languages are different. Translators often get stumped.

When the Japanese read Chinese characters they put in arrows and symbols to change the word order, according to Morita. The Chinese read the same passage directly and understand the meaning immediately. English is the same kind of language, where one reads one word after another and the meaning is immediately clear. "So we have to remember that the Americans have a different thought process; it is a linear sequence," Morita says in the Japanese version of *The Japan That Can Say No*. "Regardless of the quality of the interpreter, it is impossible to translate a thought from Japanese into English in the same sequential order." He recognizes that the Japanese thought process is in a minority. And when they communicate with Occidentals, if they don't change their thought sequences to match the Westerners', the Japanese simply will not be understood. "This is a definite disadvantage to thinking in Japanese, and we have to be aware of it."

"The physical differences between Japanese and Americans will always exist, and all we can do in that area is try to overcome them with good manners," Morita says in the most reasonable tones used in his book. However, the important problem is the current trade imbalance with the United States. If it is not rectified, Morita is aware, the Americans will continue to believe that Japan is the problem. Therefore, he believes the solution is to increase Japanese manufacturing in America and to improve export sales from America of Japanese products. Here, Morita has finally recognized the heart of the problem, and if he and his compatriots will forget public relations campaigns and stick to concrete actions geared toward rebuilding the manufacturing and export base in America, all signs of anti-Japanese feelings will most likely disappear.

CHAPTER SEVEN
America Lacks
Business Creativity

Which country invented television, VCRs, video cameras, stereo-phonic sound systems, semiconductors, computers, and even the concept of modern telecommunications? The United States.

Then why are there no more TVs, VCRs, video cameras or stereos made in the United States? Americans invented these products. Americans should dominate these markets and all the high-paid, skilled jobs that go along with them. What happened? According to the Central Intelligence Agency, Japan shipped 15 percent of the microelectronic products in the free world in 1980. By 1988, that figure had risen to 25 percent. In the same period the U.S. market share dropped from 21 percent to 17 percent. Why?

In 1980 the Japanese shipped only six percent of the West's computers. But by 1988 that figure had risen to 22 percent, a growth of 358 percent. The U.S. share of that market, over the same years, fell from 55.2 percent to 35.8 percent. In telecommunications equipment the U.S. share fell from 12.4 percent to 10.7 percent, while the Japanese market share rose from 11.7 percent to 32.7 percent. For these few industries, these figures represent lost revenues to U.S. industry in the amount of nearly 40 billion dollars per year, or 98 percent of its 1991 trade deficit with Japan. The United States lost not only its market share, but also the growth that was available in the market.

Part of the reason for this dismal performance on the part of American manufacturers, is the practice of Japanese piracy of Western technology. Part of the answer also lies in the Japanese practice of dumping their goods at below-cost prices in foreign markets in order to destroy competitors and to capture the market. But this is not the whole answer. It is perhaps not even the primary explanation for Japanese marketing preeminence amongst all high technology industries. Yet, when American and European business executives complain, one would think that these are the only reasons for Japan's success. But it isn't true.

There is another factor at work here, so subtle that it has largely escaped the attention of both Western governments and businesses. Morita reminds us in his book that the transistor and the semiconductor were both invented at America's Bell Laboratories. During his visit to Bell Labs, Morita praised the scientists for their important "academic" research. However, he told them that in any significant, practical sense, their work has been a failure. "Two other types of creativity are needed to make any invention worth the expense," he said.

The first is the ability to see how a new invention or new technology can be used. Even more, it is the ability to see how it can be used in mass production and in many applications. Morita calls this "product planning and production creativity."

The second type of creativity required is in marketing. What good is it to manufacture something if you can't sell it? Marketing, in Morita's opinion, is a vital and creative skill that the Americans seem to have lost. Perhaps he has a point. Americans used to be known around the world as Yankee Traders, but this is a name now reserved for folklore.

By contrast, Morita wants us to believe, the strength of Japanese industry is seeing the product applications available in all forms of new inventions and technologies. The Japanese rely on others to provide the new inventions, but only when others fail to make use of the idea does Japan display its real talents. Turning technology into products is where Japan is without equal in the world. Then, he huffs, Japan is also expert at getting the products sold.

Morita's comments cannot be dismissed as Japanese chauvinism. When one looks at the amount of money spent on research and development in both the United States and Japan, it begins to dawn on one that something is amiss with the American system. From 1968 to 1978, the amount of money spent on research and development in the United States, as a percentage of gross national product, fell annually from about 2.75 percent to about 2.1 percent before beginning to rise again to 2.6 percent in 1988. Over these years, the United States outspent Japan in total dollars by huge amounts for research and development. In fact, it wasn't until 1985 that Japan even passed the United States in R & D spending as a percentage of GNP.[1]

It is not that the United States is ignoring R & D.[2] To this day, the U.S. spends more money than Japan on it. Complicating the calculations on how much is spent is the fact that the American government, unlike the Japanese, spends huge amounts on research. But the results often end up in the public domain, free to anyone who can read a scientific journal.

The problem with America's research spending is that most of the allocated money is funnelled to its universities and think tank institutions like Bell Labs, where the mentality is geared to intellectual advancement. Certainly, this work is essential and it must go on. However an attitude problem exists here, and it is important to recognize it.

Universities are supposed to pursue academic excellence. But when the bulk of a country's research and development is being done by universities, a snobbishness develops that works to the detriment of the nation. Professors and graduate students do not see the value of commercial research projects. These projects are seen as anti-intellectual and do nothing to advance a professor's career. They may even be seen as compromising a university's independence.

The Japanese, on the other hand, are conducting the overwhelming part of their research within private companies. Naturally, their research takes on a more commercial aspect. When basic research is needed, the Japanese go to American universities and buy it there. It is much cheaper that way, because the United States government so heavily subsidizes university research programs. At the Massachusetts Institute of Technology, for a $10,000 fee, the Materials Processing Center's research findings are available to anybody. In this laboratory some of the most advanced work in the world is being done on high-strength ceramics and composite metals. Between 20 percent and 25 percent of MIT's customers are Japanese companies.

The emphasis at a Japanese company is on research and development that will aid the company. If the work also advances scientific knowledge, that's fine, but it's not the goal. This difference in research philosophy forces a difference in the points of view of those who work on the projects. Japanese engineers and scientists are devoted to developing the more easily manufactured processes with the most cost-effective methods. Too many American engineers tend to focus on an engineering or scientific point of view rather than manufacturing efficiency and marketing.

The result is that the Japanese have found more efficient ways to produce televisions, VCRs, semiconductors and automobiles, and have for years been knocking the Americans out of one market after another. In esoteric fields, such as X-ray lithography which prints complex circuits on semiconductors, the Japanese have swamped the U.S. with development programs by a ratio of five-to-one.[3] Is it any wonder that Americans lose the benefit of inventions when they fail in the follow-up?

The most thankless job in America has to be that of an inventor. A job that should be lauded and celebrated across the land is instead frequently ridiculed: an inventor is an oddball, an eccentric. The world gives awards for intellectual achievement, but nothing for practical genius. Morita of Sony offers an interesting example of this peculiarity. When Sony brought the transistor back to Japan from Bell Labs in the early 1950s, a Mr. Esaki, one of Sony's researchers, discovered how to use it in a small radio. Later, this man took a job at IBM where his work in basic research won him a Nobel prize. He won nothing for developing the transistor radio.

Why isn't there more commercial research and development going on in America? Some Americans complain that product liability laws make new products too expensive to introduce. They are afraid of being sued. Some complain about the overly protective patent and copyright laws, that a company risks enormous liability if it even looks at an inventor's letter of introduction for a new product. It seems that corporate America is more afraid of litigation than of going out of business for a lack of new product introductions. They seem content to give the old products a new paint job, or to cut prices to extend their product's market life.

The danger of being sued should not simply be dismissed out of hand, because it is a definite risk of doing business in America. The United States in inundated with lawyers trying to make a living. For every 100,000 people in American there are 281 lawyers versus 111 in Germany, 82 in the United Kingdom and eleven in Japan.[4]

But the pertinent fact is that research costs money. If a company doesn't do any research this quarter, the savings will fall directly to the bottom line, and this quarter's profits will show an increase over last year. The manager will look like a hero and get a bonus. Unfortunately, his or her successor may have to file for bankruptcy.

In 1990, the Big Three American automobile manufacturers purchased 400,000 Japanese cars. But that same year, the Big Three sold only 24,000 cars to Japan. This fact is seen as American marketing laziness in Japan. The Japanese do not understand why they are criticized for selling so many of their products in America. They did not ask the Detroit car makers to buy their products. "Doesn't Detroit have its own development programs?" they ask.

The Japanese want to know how a nation can be criticized for working too hard and for planning ahead. Is it their fault if the world prefers Japanese quality? Do they force Americans to buy Japanese cameras? Do the Americans or Europeans make quality products at reasonable prices? In the opinion of most Japanese leaders today, apparently not. According to Morita, there are very few products made in America that the Japanese want to buy, and that is the heart of the trade deficit problem. Japan is not selling too much. America is buying too much.

Morita said in his book that if America would get back into business instead of sitting on its laurels, the trade problem would vanish. The same is true for most of Europe. If the Europeans want to correct trade imbalances, they ought to start producing goods that are saleable not only in Japan, but also in their own countries. It is in this area, says Morita, that Japanese politicians ought to begin telling the Americans and Europeans where to get off. "They need to find a little backbone to stand up to our (Japan's) trading partners."[5]

When the Reagan Administration's Secretary of Commerce Robert Verity, traveled to Japan with 25 representatives of U.S. companies to sell their products, Morita was the person who greeted them. Morita told them that he would be happy to provide any help he could. In addition, he said that he had been selling his products in the United States for 30 years and the Japanese Minister of International Trade and Industry never needed to accompany him. Morita asked if it was Verity's intention to create an "America, Incorporated." Secretary Verity only smiled, but the American businessmen all laughed out loud.

One of the Americans in the Verity group asked Morita why the Japanese government supported its businesses. Morita replied that "the government does not own stock in business." But his company pays over 50 percent of its profits in taxes. "If business does not do well, then the government cannot provide the services that the nation expects. Therefore, the government looks on business as a partner. In America, the government is seen as interfering, and business is seen as rapacious. It's a shame they can't get together."[6]

Part of Morita's complaints, however, are merely self-serving. The truth of the matter is that the Japanese get away with marketing tactics that would land any American executive in jail. In the United States, it's against the law to sell products for less than their manufacturing cost when the purpose is to gain a marketing advantage over your competitors. Yet, the Japanese have been employing that tactic for years. Here, it's called dumping.

Zenith Electronics has spent a fortune in a futile 12-year lobbying battle to curb dumping in the television market. In 1990, lawyers representing flat-panel electronic display screen manufacturers filed a complaint against the Japanese for dumping. Their petition charges that Toshiba, Matsushita Electric, Hitachi and Sharp are selling products at far less than either the home prices in Japan or the manufacturing costs.

The American semiconductor industry has nearly been destroyed by Japanese dumping. After years of wrangling over the issue of microprocessor patents and pricing, Motorola finally gave up its court fight with Hitachi, Ltd. It was too expensive to continue the struggle. Micro Computer Supply, Inc., an American company that sells computer diskettes and other supplies, recently sued Hitachi's Maxell subsidiary and TDK Electronics (both Japanese) for discriminatory pricing practices.

Since 1985 Honeywell has had a running battle going with Minolta Camera to prevent exports of certain camera equipment to the United States. Honeywell's suit says it provided Minolta with technical information for making auto-focus modules with the understanding that Minolta would then use Honeywell's products. It charges that Minolta used that information to set up a parallel development program. It then began competing with Honeywell by introducing its own products. The courts will eventually decide these issues, but the stories are not new. We have been hearing similar tales for years.

Zenith Electronics is also involved in a bet-the-company development effort in high-definition television (HDTV). Its major competitors are, of course, Japanese. The problem Zenith faces is financing development with a business that is barely profitable. It must also secure from the U.S. government approval for its technology and some assurance that it will be adopted as the national standard. That will protect Zenith for awhile from outside competition which is working along different technological lines. Zenith worries that if Japanese technology is allowed to set the standard for America, dumping will not be the issue. Zenith will have wasted its development efforts and will lose its competitive position in this new industry. Japanese lobbying efforts in Washington are intense, and this issue is still not settled.

Every once in a while, though, the tables are turned. On July 12, 1990, a tiny company in California's Silicon Valley, Conductus, Inc., announced that it would become the world's first plant dedicated to making superconducting chips, and began production the following day. Hewlett-Packard has a stake in this company and has been getting the first test-run products.

If Conductus is smart, though, it will avoid the sure-to-be-offered joint ventures with Japanese companies. Today, one of the most costly errors that Western companies can make today is to mistake Japanese largesse, in terms of development capital, as something beneficial. The Japanese do not take partners. They take hostages. They operate on the age-old, feudal marriage theory: What's yours is mine and what's mine is mine. The Japanese are never the bride; it's their partners who bring the dowry.

General Electric also seems to be having some success in converting its research scientists from pure academicians to innovators mindful of commercial possibilities. But it's now high time that the rest of American and European businesses realize that their marketing people are not the only source of new product ideas. In fact, the best source is probably their laboratories. These scientists need to be encouraged to see the applicability of their ideas in the world of manufacturing and consumption.

There is one other aspect of the decline of America's economic power that needs to be explored. It exists in America's relationships with countries around the world. Economic power has given the United States enormous international clout over the years. Often, in the past, the United States government just had to speak to recalcitrant Third World countries to get them to settle their local disputes, civil rights violations or trade wars. Sometimes, however, America felt it had to take more forcible actions.

It can be argued whether or not the United States ever had any right to such power, but morality is not the issue here. The point is that for good or ill America led the West during the entire Cold War period. Its economy and its weapons provided the Western might.

A fundamental principle should be understood here. The United States did not rise to its position of world economic and political leadership because it had more aircraft carriers and missiles. Rather, it achieved that position because it had the steel mills and factories that could produce these armaments. World leadership was not based on the nebulous benefits of a service economy.

If America wants to regain preeminent world stature, the United States will have to take the measures required to rebuild its manufacturing economy. The message ought to be clear by now: Free trade is what you give away when you can't handle all the business yourself. The Japanese understand this important principle even if nobody else does.

Take a look at something as innocent appearing as foreign aid. Back in 1989, Japan became the largest contributor nation on earth. But, contrary to most Western countries' policy, almost none of it was grant money. Japan didn't give a dime to any country that didn't reciprocate in some way. Grants were only given when a payment in either a favor, cash or trade was expected.

The Japanese and the countries that receive the aid, jointly build power plants or shoe factories or new mines. Part of the aid package is an agreement that Japan will take a share of the

electricity to support their local factories. They will take a share
of the shoes or logs or fish that their investment helped to produce. They want the production from the mines that their aid
developed, and they want it at costs that are negotiated favorably.
All construction materials, parts, management talent and shipping are supplied by Japanese sources. Nothing is spent without
prior lender approval.

FOREIGN AID SPENDING IN 1989[7]
(in billions of dollars)

Japan	$9.0
United States	$7.7
France	$5.1
Germany	$5.0
Italy	$3.3
Britain	$2.6
Canada	$2.3

The essential relationships depicted in the above foreign aid
chart are mostly unchanged in 1992. What's important is to get a
bearing on the points in time when American leadership began to
slip.

The Japanese have also learned that when their environmental excesses become too much for the world to stomach, they
can let contracts out for the work. Taiwan never had the enormous driftnets that cover 35 miles of ocean at a single placement
until the Japanese helped it get into the business. The Japanese
wanted the fish, and they wanted them caught economically, so
they gave assistance to the Taiwanese who are better able to take
the heat from the international community.

The same thing is true of hardwood-cutting in the Southeast Asian rain forests. Japan takes as many raw logs from these delicate ecosystems as does the whole of Europe. Although the United States has to take its share of the heat for despoiling those forests, there is at least a growing protectionist sentiment in this country that is curbing its participation. The destruction of those giant trees that took hundreds of years to mature, and that are so needed for maintenance of the earth's atmosphere, is heavily supported by Japanese foreign aid.[8] With their own resources, the local people of Borneo and Sumatra could never have afforded the equipment to clear those forests, nor did they have the managerial talent to supervise the operation. The Japanese provided both and are now receiving their payment in logs. When the forests are destroyed, the Sumatrans will each own a Sony television and a patch of barren land. They will wonder what happened to their jobs and what they will do next year when the forest is gone and no longer providing sustenance.

Unlike American or European aid, Japanese aid payments are not part of a broad democratic discussion process. Their payments are decided by a narrow coterie of politicians within the Liberal Democratic Party who have specific national investment goals in mind. Naoki Tanaka, a Japanese economist, said in *Gekkan Asahi* magazine that "there has been little discussion of how the world's biggest creditor should behave."[9]

It is ominous that the United States should have lost its position as the largest contributor to foreign aid. America's gross national product is still almost twice as large as Japan's. The difference is that today much less of the GNP is in the form of manufactured goods than it was a decade ago. It was by manufacturing that the United States was able to generate income at a level sufficient to keep up the responsibilities of a major industrial nation. It is important to see the relationship between growing real incomes (noninflationary income) and the country's ability to generate tax dollars for national programs.

The American economy today is, like any service economy, essentially inflationary by nature. The pattern is to import more and more products and become more and more service-oriented. Because it manufactures less, there are fewer export opportunities. This is true regardless of the improving U.S. balance of trade over the past few years. America is exporting grain, logs, ore and other raw materials, not job and wealth producing manufactured goods.[10] The United States' trade deficit in 1991 was 66 billion dollars, a 35 percent improvement over 1990 and the first time in many years that the deficit did not exceed 100 billion dollars.

During the first 30 years after World War II manufacturing represented a higher portion of the United States GNP and there was a positive trade balance. The country was also producing enough jobs every year so that the problems of homelessness, drug addiction and crime were not as severe as they are today.

The result of becoming more of a service economy is constant trade deficits financed by selling bonds to the foreign countries which are shipping those products. The deeper in debt the United States goes, the higher the interest rate that has to be paid to foreigners who hold its bonds. The higher interest rates raise the cost of financing everything else from the cost of owning a home to purchasing an automobile or building a new factory.

This scenario demonstrates vividly how little service-produced profits are worth in the overall structure of a nation. They are not capital formation dollars. Service-produced profits are returned to the economy either to produce more service, which is ephemeral, or to pay dividends or, in the final phase of economic decadence, to pay the cost of importing the products needed for survival and formerly produced domestically.

Service industry profits are inflation-producing dollars whose lack of value derives from not having created something tangible. Service industries are the enemy of manufacturers when they compete for capital or labor. In a society that is conscious of its need for capital formation, the tax structure should reflect a bias in favor of manufacturing and offer additional incentives for exporting.

The only real wealth the United States produces as a nation comes from its factories. America's growing inability to keep up with charitable aid at home or abroad is a direct reflection of its declining manufacturing sector. The Japanese are correct to criticize America for lacking in business creativity. If the United States can't understand the basic principles of capitalism, it will never grasp the finer points of product and market development.

The drumbeat being heard in America today is a dirge. It is a slow march to the gallows. It is not too late to change the rhythm, but time is short. Leaders are needed in Washington and in corporate boardrooms who must set aside personal greed and chart a path for an economic renaissance. But crippling greed, in all likelihood, will not disappear until a sufficiently oppressive tax burden on personal wealth is instituted. Then America can begin to fight back.

CHAPTER EIGHT
MAKOTO: Purity of Purpose

On June 17, 1990, at the Consumer Electronics Show in Chicago, Morita told *The New York Times'* columnist, Hans Fantel, that he had no plans to retire. Instead, Sony's Chairman of the Board, at age 69, announced that he was taking on an additional responsibility. "I'm going to be the company philosopher," he said.

"Particularly in a highly technical enterprise, philosophy is vital," said Morita. "It is needed to place technical developments and products within the entire texture of modern social existence. The philosopher must see technology in its human context so as to guide the aims of engineering."[1]

If Morita's comments sound like the Japanese version of something that might be printed in an American company's annual report or like public relations department hypergloss, then you have missed a fundamental concept of what makes a Japanese company successful. Morita's comment is an application of *makoto*, or purity of purpose. *Makoto* is the philosophy behind Shintoism, which is the basis of much of Japanese culture. Unfortunately, Shintoism resolves all interpersonal issues within a rigid hierarchal system of duty. It is a male-dominated society, regardless of the few women who have made some newsworthy political headlines in Japan. It works to the detriment of all other nations, because Shintoism is a Japan-first religion. The danger of *makoto*, therefore, is that what begins in innocence and simplicity often becomes arrogance.

Morita is seen almost as a visionary in Japan, a person whose contributions to Sony, and to Japanese business in general, have lifted him to the status of a modern shogun. To understand his status, one considerably more important than that which Lee Iococca of Chrysler holds in America, an understanding of *bushido* is essential. This is the code of conduct that the old samurais lived under before the Meiji Restoration in 1868. It establishes the Japanese hierarchy and the individual's responsibility to society.

Bushido and Shintoism are two sides of the same coin. You cannot define one without reference to the other. To say that the ideals of *bushido* have been dead since the MacArthur Constitution is like saying that Christianity died in the Soviet Union when the Communists took over. It just isn't so. *Bushido* is as much a part of the Japanese psyche today as it was when Nippon was ruled by the shoguns. The allegiances are the same: To Emperor Akihito, to Japan, to the company and to the family, in that order.

Morita has achieved a position somewhere between that of a revered politician and company president, a rare accomplishment in Japan. He is as famous as most prime ministers and is treated as if he had all the answers, or at least as if his contribution could make a great difference. People in Japan do not dispute him. The doctrine of *bushido* gives him a position of respect that is almost never achieved by businesspeople in other countries. This is so because, "the Japanese concentrate on the material benefits far more than any abstract moral or political principles. There is no principle other than money itself."[2] And Morita has done an outstanding job building Sony. He has done all that *bushido* requires of him.

"Japan is a society where the struggle for economic power is paramount...The group, and by extension Japan, must win at any cost. Any tactic is acceptable."[3] These are strong words, but they accurately describe Japan in the Twentieth Century.

It helps us to understand why the Japanese are compulsive workaholics when we know that it is an integral part of Shintoism. Within his group, each person works to make his emperor and Japan preeminent in the world. At the top are the shoguns, some in business, some in the government, and some in the military, who set the direction for the *corpus nipponica*. They strive for a purity of purpose that will keep them on a straight path towards their goal of world economic dominance. Deviations from the path are unpatriotic, and governments succeed or fall based on their ability to support the plan.

Japan's success is partly due to its belief that in order to take over as the dominant force in any industry, several issues have to be attacked simultaneously: New or improved products, manufacturing, distribution and customer service. By concentrating national efforts on single industries, the Japanese have been able to rise from niche marketers to dominance in one industry after another.

In addition, the Japanese have made certain that priority takeovers occur in key industries such as machine tools. Loss of American control of machine tool production in the United States, for example, threatens its future competitiveness. In the 1980s, Japan and Germany, along with a few other countries, captured 49 percent of U.S. sales of machine tools. Orders for American tools fell 22 percent in 1989 alone while Japan was enjoying a 33 percent sales increase.[4]

Part of the problem is that the American manufacturing effort has been handicapped for the past 20 years by disappearing apprenticeship programs and schools that graduate subliterate workers with no concept of either discipline or work ethics. When American schools lost the power to control dress codes, and to enforce rules of conduct, and then gave up on rote, mechanical learning—such as the multiplication tables, and veered away from vocational training, they doomed a whole generation of ordinary people to a life of underemployment. The cream of the crop can often rise on its own regardless of the educational system, but the masses need more guidance and preparation. They aren't getting it.

In Japan, because they are better prepared, employees feel as if they have more at stake in the company and take pride in their jobs. A story that Ishihara tells is an excellent illustration of this. A woman assembly line worker at Nippon Electric Corporation (NEC) observed that her plant was having sporadic quality problems with semiconductors. She observed that the bad ones tended to come from the same batches and that intervening batches were uniformly good products. One day she noticed that the plant floor vibrated as a nearby train whizzed by, and reasoned that this might have an adverse affect on the semiconductors. When she informed the plant supervisor, he saw immediately that this disturbance might indeed cause the delicate machinery to produce defects. He had a large ditch dug between the railroad tracks and the plant, and then filled it with water. The result was a drastic decline in the number of defects.

The United States' budget deficits in the 1980s and early 1990s have made borrowing expensive, and that hurts business growth. The decline in real personal income lowers the savings rate, and this reduces the fund of investment capital. America's lack of a national strategic plan for economic redevelopment means that enormous sums of money are wasted on corporate takeovers and leveraged buyouts, rather than being spent on new product development.

However, America has to remember that Japan rose to its current position from the depths of a war-torn, bombed-out shell. The U.S. can make a comeback. Companies like Honda succeeded by concentrating on improving the manufacturing process. Kent Bowen, co-director of the Leaders for Manufacturing program at MIT, said recently, "A U.S. company puts two-thirds of its effort into developing a product and one-third into developing the manufacturing process. The Japanese and Germans reverse those ratios."[5]

In U.S. industry there is something called the 15/80 rule which says that 80 percent of a product's cost is determined in the first 15 percent of its development cycle. Unless the design engineers are working with their production people from the start, a project can go through numerous redesigns and billowing cost overruns.

American businesses would gain from combining their design engineering and production departments, as Japan does now. This is referred to as concurrent engineering, and it has saved enormous amounts of time and expense on the front-end of the new product development process.

The production process in Japan is also different in that factories react quickly to their customers' requests. Japan manufactures on demand in small batches. Its suppliers are geared to deliver parts only when needed and on very short notice, and inventories are thus kept to a minimum. This process is called just-in-time manufacturing. It was designed by Taiichi Ono, a former executive vice president for production at Toyota.

By contrast, the United States depends on long production lead times, heavy inventories, giant production runs and standardized products. Customer service is usually only given lip service. Job shops, where products are made-to-order in small quantities, are associated with mom and pop delicatessens and are not thought to have anything to do with real manufacturing operations.

There are, however, a few American corporations that have seen the light and are changing over to the Japanese manufacturing system. Caterpillar Tractor is probably the most notable success story. After spending over two billion dollars in redesigning its factories in East Peoria, Illinois, Caterpillar now has the capability of producing multiple product lines concurrently. Job set-up and tear-down time has been reduced from hours or days to minutes. Computers control tool selections and guide the cutting operations. Waste and scrap problems have been largely eliminated as a result, and for the first time in years, Caterpillar is now competitive with Komatsu, its Japanese counterpart. It remains to be seen, however, if Caterpillar will continue with this heavy reinvestment strategy or allow itself to slip back into the more comfortable mode of aiming for big dividends, high management salaries, and masterminding stock buyback schemes. Caterpillar certainly hasn't learned any lessons in labor relations and is in real danger of losing the company entirely if management can't find a common ground with labor.

The last manufacturing difference that should be mentioned is America's continuing heavy reliance on draftsmen who still make blueprints on paper. In this day of computer-aided design and manufacturing systems, it seems incredible that any company would waste so much valuable time on such an antiquated system. This operation would be seen in Japan as a complete deviation from *makoto*.

In the United States, attention to customer needs is often slip-shod. Department stores and other retailers tend to have fairly good reputations for customer service, yet manufacturers, especially automobile makers, have a checkered history. It often takes consumer group complaints, congressional and insurance company prodding, and the enforcement of Transportation Department regulations before any action is taken to make auto safety changes. For example, General Motors' 1987 Buicks, Oldsmobiles and Pontiacs had engines that quit running at awkward times, but they were not recalled until 1992, and then from original owners only.

Chrysler, to its credit, finally added driver's side airbags to some of its cars, an innovation now featured in their advertisements. Chrysler also deserves some applause for its seven-year drive train warranty. Even so, it is difficult to understand why Chrysler and other automobile makers are not trying to make the Japanese look like anemic also-rans. If Americans aren't going to protect their home market, where do they plan to do battle? American businesses don't seem to understand that they are in a fight for their existence. This is no time for a dividends-as-usual policy. Only the recession of 1991-92, and the consequent slump in sales, forced the Detroit automobile manufacturers to scale back their dividends—not any perceived need to retool or to reorganize.

Perhaps it's only that the Japanese get better press coverage, but they seem to scoop their world counterparts in public relations, and have built a solid image for quality. Take Honda, which is supplying its dealers worldwide with devices to retrieve chlorofluorocarbons. (This dangerous gas, which depletes ozone from the atmosphere, is normally allowed to escape from automobile air-conditioners during servicing.) Honda and its dealers will foot the bill for the device (priced at 1,680 dollars each). Yet the cost of service will not increase. With this move, Honda scored some important environmental points and did so without being commercially crass.

The Honda safety upgrade is a good example of an important Japanese business strategy: A company seeking acceptance in the market in which it operates. The Japanese know that it's easier to sell in an atmosphere of good will. That's why important new product announcements, especially in consumer goods, are always made by their best spokesmen. That's why Morita himself, in 1990, announced the introduction of Sony's Digital Audio Tapes (DATs).

It seems that you can't open the newspaper without learning of yet another new product development from Japan. This is the most obvious manifestation of *makoto*. Japanese business is dedicated to producing a constant flow of high quality new products at reasonable prices. They are overwhelming the West with their purity of purpose.

For example, Nippon Telegraph & Telephone Corporation recently announced a new optic-memory material capable of high-speed information retrieval and greater information-storage capacity. They claim this material is 100 million times faster than existing optical-storage materials.

Hitachi introduced software that will allow Chinese-made terminals to hook up with Hitachi's computers. They did this to make it easier to compete with other brands. Hitachi will now have the only computer that will work with Chinese terminals. The China Greatwall Computer Group, in addition, will become an information sharing partner with Hitachi on all business ventures with Western clients. This improvement in customer service may add millions of dollars to Hitachi's coffers over the years from the information flow alone.

When Japanese businesses have quality problems, such as Toyota's cruise control malfunctions with its Lexus sedan, they react with proper care and concern. Toyota notified every Lexus owner and offered to repair the car on the spot if the customer brought the car to the dealer. Otherwise, Toyota arranged to pick up the car and repair it over-night and return it ready-to-go the next morning. In either case, the defect was not only fixed, the car was washed, vacuumed and filled with gasoline. Toyota, in redressing the problem so quickly and efficiently, demonstrated again how serious it is about capturing and holding on to its foreign market shares.

Even for its more modestly priced cars Toyota servicing is becoming legend. Each repair shop is divided into red teams and blue teams. They compete with each other for promptness of work and for the fewest customer complaints. The system works well, as most Toyota owners can tell you.

Japan is also fiercely protective of its home markets, and hates to allow any foreign competition to disrupt traditional distribution patterns. During ex-Commerce Secretary Robert Verity's visit to Japan with representatives from 25 American manufacturers, Ishihara reports that he and Verity engaged in a harsh exchange. An agreement had just been reached that called for an American company's participation in the second construction phase at Haneda airport. When Verity offered his thanks for Japan's allowing an American company to participate, Ishihara got angry and told Verity that this would be the last time that he would allow his country to cave in to American pressure.

Ishihara says that the United States has put unreasonable pressure on Japan for having a closed market in large construction projects. Apparently, however, the pressure hasn't worked, for there has only been one American construction company licensed to work in Japan. But Ishihara denies that Japan's restrictions on registering foreign construction firms are severe. He believes that any company that really wants to operate in Japan can find a way to meet the requirements.

Ishihara, in his book, also cites poor relations between the Commerce Department and the U.S. Trade Representative's office. He says, "they quarrel like dogs and monkeys and are always saying bad things about each other. It's obvious that America will never get its trade policy together."[6] In the official translation, he says, "From this side of the Pacific, we tend to think of the U.S. government as a powerful monolith. That is not the case."[7] His point is that if the United States could get itself organized it might do better at selling its products in Japan.

In spite of the impediments, a few American companies have had some success in breaking into the Japanese market. Motorola won a 35 million dollar annual contract to install a mobile cellular-phone network in the Tokyo area. Even better, Motorola was subsequently selected to provide the digital voice technology for Japan's next generation telephone system. Participating in this development program for Nippon Telegraph & Telephone are two other foreign companies: American Telephone & Telegraph, along with Telephon AB L.M. Ericsson of Sweden. It's not a lot of business at this point, and there is a risk that all the program will do is give away technology. But all three companies believe that the chance to build a long-term relationship that would lead to more opportunities in the future makes the project worthwhile.

Following are a few more examples of ostensible openings in the Japanese market. At face value they would seem to contradict the philosophy of *makoto* which demands that Japan protect and nurture its own industries to the exclusion of foreigners. But one needs to look for the reality behind the facade of promises.

Toyota announced in the summer of 1990 that it would buy up to 94 million dollars worth of U.S. semiconductors for their world wide automobile production facilities. This action would have lifted the U.S. share of Toyota's semiconductor purchases from 2.1 percent in 1989 to 10.9 percent in 1992. Every little bit helps, and it is nice to hear that the Japanese, in this case, had momentarily stopped complaining about U.S. quality. However, it hasn't happened.

As for the Japanese semiconductor market in total, there is an agreement between the United States and Japan that allows foreigners to share up to 20 percent of this 20 billion dollar a year business. The American share of the Japanese semiconductor market had grown from 8.5 percent in 1985 to 14 percent in 1989, but subsequently, the 20 percent by July 1990 goal was not met. The Japanese asked for a delay of one year, and in return promised that the goal could be extended to 30 percent of the market. The 20 percent target was not reached in 1991 either, and in 1992 there will undoubtedly be another new excuse.

Just as likely, though, is the probability that Japan will spend the additional year(s) buying up U.S. semiconducter manufacturers or their factories. That way, Japan would be able to control any new import business. It would be like taking a yen out of one pocket and putting it into another. In fact, the request of a one-year delay was followed a few months later by a Matsushita Electric Industrial Corporation announcement that it was negotiating to buy the former Fairchild semiconductor plant in Puyallup, Washington. This is the same plant that received so much attention in Congress when Fujitsu Ltd. attempted to buy it a year before.

Fairchild (now National Semiconductor Corporation) said that it was giving up on trying to manufacture a one-megabit static random access memory chip in the plant. S-RAMs retain information even when the electricity is turned off. They are used in portable computers, facsimile machines, video cameras and a wide range of other consumer electronic products. Previously, Motorola and VLSI Technology had both tried to produce this chip but they are now also out of this market.

What these examples demonstrate is that there is more than one way to skin a cat. If one Japanese company can't buy a factory in the U.S., a second company still may. Matsushita bought the Fairchild plant in February 1991 and gained a priceless technological advantage. A Japanese purchaser often just has to wait for the heat to cool down. And on the American side, the doctrine of short-term profits must be protected even if it costs the country its long-term ability to compete in the world of high technology. The United States will be able to export more chips to Japan. But the chips won't be its own.

In another case, Businessland, America's largest dealer in personal computers, decided that the only practical way to enter the Japanese market was to sell part of its stock to Japanese partners. Canon, Fujitsu, Sony and Toshiba now own five percent each of the Businessland (Japan) enterprise. Softbank Corporation, a Japanese distributor, owns 26 percent of the company. Hopefully, Businessland knows what it is doing. Computerland, the last American company to enter the Japanese market eventually had to sell its 30 stores to Japanese investors. They could not compete against the local distribution networks. Businessland, in all likelihood, is simply providing store operating procedures and merchandising guidance for its future Japanese owners.

In fact, the only real merchandising success that the United States has had in Japan is not in store operations, but in name brand apparel. The Japanese love Ralph Lauren's "Polo" line. The United States has captured 7.5 percent of the Japanese apparel market, with Polo accounting for the largest chunk. And as you might expect, a lot of Ralph Lauren's fabrics are made in Japan and sewn in South Korea or Taiwan, not in the United States.

Toys "R" Us opened its second store in Japan in January 1992—President George Bush was on hand for the inauguration—and believes that it has overcome the local, small shop syndicates that in the past have controlled large store retailing. It remains to be seen if it will have any success operating a 45,000 square foot store in Japan. The company sold a 20 percent share of the company to Den Fujita, who owns the McDonalds franchise in Japan, and that assistance may help Toys "R" Us avoid trouble from the small shop owners. However, the traditional middlemen who, in Japan, are placed between the wholesaler and the retailer may still present a problem of resupply for Toys "R" Us, because they have a lot of control over imports, and their primary customers are the small shop owners.

There is a certain cooperation that exists in Japan between all the various layers of retailing, warehouses, distributors and manufacturers. These businesses belong to associations and syndicates that are determined to promote and protect Japanese business interests. American retailers will have a tough time countering this well-established business culture. It's not like the free-for-all system in the West where anybody with a better idea can succeed. *Makoto*, a Japan-first philosophy, rules in Nippon.

CHAPTER NINE

Human Rights And Labor Relations

One of the many changes that took place as a result of the Allies' imposing a new constitution on Japan and the subsequent democratization of the Imperial government was the abolition of slave labor. Prior to World War II, most Japanese workers held a status only marginally better than that of feudal serfs. These workers had almost no freedom to change jobs or organize labor unions. And the unions that did exist had little affect on either business or government policy. The use of Korean slave labor was extensive, and in their occupied territories, local peoples were forced into factories and mines to work under miserable conditions for coolie wages.

General Douglas MacArthur changed the way in which the Japanese think about business and labor law. His impact on modern Japan is incomparable. MacArthur's influence led to legislation that barred workers' layoffs even in hard times without extensive notice and compensation. Now, 40 years later, it is nearly unheard of for a person to be fired for anything less than felonious misconduct. In addition, tax laws were redesigned to be more socially equitable.

In effect, "MacArthur created a bond between management and the workers," writes Akio Morita. "They have formed a community of common interests in order to survive. The workers know that their jobs are secure and that they cannot be fired. This gives them a comfortable sense of security, and they are anxious to protect that benefit. Workers are not stupid; they recognize a good thing when they see it. As a result, they all work together as a team knowing that they all share a common destiny, workers and managers alike. If the company fails, they all fail."

Edwin O. Reischauer, the former U.S. Ambassador to Japan, in describing this attitude among Japanese workers, states that a job in Japan is not merely a contractual arrangement for pay, but a means of identification with a larger entity—in other words, it provides a satisfying sense of being part of something big and significant.

What MacArthur created in Japan was a corporate entity that fit perfectly with historical Japanese culture. The company replaced the local shogun, or *daimyo*, of feudal days. A community of like-minded people was created, and their individual rights to job security were protected by law. It was the same as the old days, only better. The Communist unions that had begun to spring up so disruptively in pre-War Japan now became minor annoyances.

In these Japanese fate-sharing corporations, managerial attitudes are dramatically different from those in most Western companies. Japanese managers know that they are going to have their employees with them for the rest of their careers, so they take special pains to see that employees are well-trained and understand why certain routines are followed. Many company presidents in Japan today were in fact once union leaders. The goal is for employees to feel as if they have spent a useful and rewarding life by the time they reach retirement age, and to feel that their work was appreciated. As a result, most Japanese workers have a great sense of team spirit.

Because union leaders in Japan have equal opportunity to reach the top of corporate management, they too feel as if they were part of the same team. Consequently, union leaders almost always support the goals and policies of the company. They don't pursue myopic, short-term goals. They share the executives' belief that the best long-range policy is to set aside reinvestment money for new capital equipment and plant modernization. They learn the benefits of compromise and understand that the world is their competitor. Unions do not have to be told that Japanese products must be priced accordingly to compete in a world market with other Asian, American and European goods. Moreover, they believe they are a part of the team.

By contrast, labor laws and attitudes in the United States have been established by strife on the picket lines and in the courts. Labor-management relations in America, as in the United Kingdom, were built on the adversarial precepts of common law. Take whatever you can get away with, and the devil take the hindmost.

According to the Japanese, and to many Latin Americans for that matter, the United States is being hypocritical when it rails at South Africa for its human rights violations. Which is the bigger crime? They argue that denying South African blacks the right to vote and laying-off American workers are equally reprehensible. How can American companies expect employee loyalty when so often, after many years of loyal service, employees are turned out on the streets with no guaranteed income beyond a paltry, short-term welfare check?

Criticizing America in these circumstances is complicated. The United States never seems able to blend two policies into one strategy. After the World War, the burning question was, how might it be possible to help Japan recover economically and at the same time protect American jobs? By the 1970s, the two countries were arguing over textiles, automobiles, steel and electronics. Yet, the United States always settled these disputes in Japan's favor, never once harming Japan's access to American markets. The United States paid for this even-handedness with growing unemployment in every one of those industries. Too bad, American workers were told. You aren't competitive.

France, however, saw no harm in implementing a tariff to protect its small home industries. Italy claimed quotas were necessary to protect its labor. Germany taxed anything foreign, even cheese and potatoes, and tax-clobbered any imports that were manufactured.

The British, seemingly sharing the United States' feelings of charity and brotherly love, followed America's path. Britain felt responsible for protecting the economies of its former colonies and fellow members of the British Commonwealth. Never mind that its policy of tariff-free borders nearly destroyed its home industrial base and forced British citizens onto unemployment lines.

Kenichi Ohmae, a management consultant with McKinsey & Co. in Tokyo, wrote in his latest book, *The Borderless World*, about the need to overcome the traditional nation-state mentality. He sees nothing wrong with America's free trade policies. He argues that it is the consumers who have the real power, that it is they who are driving us into interlinked economies. This is simply not true. Consumers are at the end of the product development line. They will buy the products that offer the best value regardless of the country of origin. The power therefore resides with the manufacturers whose products have found market acceptance, for they have discovered the secret to economic success.

There is no need for the United States to find itself interlinked with Japan to the extent that it supplies America with 30 percent of its automobiles, almost all of its televisions and VCRs, and many of its other consumer electronics products. America has the capability of making these products itself and would do so if these markets had not been surrendered. Interlinking the economies of Japan and the United States is a political decision, not an economic nor a consumer-driven one.

Workers and executives form an effective team in Japan. This same team spirit is not as prevalent among the individualistic Americans. The following anecdote from Joseph and Suzy Fucini's book, *Working for the Japanese*, illustrates this cleft between Japanese managers and American workers.

At a Mazda plant in Michigan, the company issued its American workers baseball caps with the Mazda logo on the front. Wearing the cap was voluntary, although wearing the company uniform of blue pants and khaki shirts was mandatory. As one might expect, the workers made up their own minds about wearing the cap. Half did, the other half left it at home. Mazda management was not happy. They felt that if the workers really cared about the company, they would want to wear the caps even if it wasn't mandatory. The Americans could understand being told what they had to do, but not what they should want to do.

Therein lies a critical difference between Japanese and American workers. The Japanese are apparently willing to be led into a corporate group identity to a far greater extent than are Americans. But American workers also can be very productive and loyal employees in return for job security. They just aren't willing to give up their individual identities in the process.

However, even in Japan there are limits to the citizens' loyalty. When the government created a new national holiday called Conjugal Day, to combat the falling birth rate, the Japanese went to work anyway.

Many Japanese executives are astounded by the salaries of their American counterparts. They see American corporate executives as immoral predators who suck the life-blood of unsuspecting workers. Moreover, American CEOs are seen as denying their workers a sense of contributing to something more important: They have no say in management's decisions, and do not share management's economic security. I agree. One of the primary causes of America's trade problems is management greed. They make decisions based on what is good for management, frequently to the detriment of the company.

Morita claims that Japanese people do not usually work for wages alone. Japanese workers have a sense of mission. They feel that there is a purpose to their work. They hold their jobs for a lifetime and develop a sense of loyalty to the company. Their work gives them an important identity that American workers seldom have. And if ever a criticism hurt, it is this one, that most American companies don't really care about their workers and that American workers have lost heart in their work.

An American company trying to create this sense of unity in the workplace should remember that loyalty to a company does not exist where there is no loyalty on the company's part to its employees. Repetitive hiring and firing and mass layoffs ruin any chance of building worker loyalty. Those workers who are left know that it is but for the grace of God they remain. They understand that their jobs are secure only until the next round of layoffs.

Government-mandated severance pay and retraining programs, as well as protected pension plans, would go a long way toward stabilizing employment in the United States. The government needs to draw up a list of acceptable reasons for dismissal for all private enterprises. As it stands now, subjective performance reviews are used to coerce senior employees into either resigning or retiring early. Performance reviews are bludgeons devised to mask management's discriminatory policies against minorities, the aging and anybody considered surplus. By amassing a file of two, three or four performance reviews over the course of six months, a company can expel an employee, regardless of the length of service, simply by saying that he or she has become uncooperative. It is also increasingly evident that new federal rules are needed to regulate executive compensation in publicly traded companies. Tax policy is no longer enough.

Morita believes that American executives think of their employees as mere tools who can be used to build profits and then discarded when no longer needed. In fact, American workers are treated worse than tools. Tools are at least oiled and stored safely on a shelf. In the United States, workers are put out on the street and given only minimal government charity to keep them from starving in public.

Heaven help the person who is suddenly out of work and over 50 years of age. In fact, if over 40 years old, that person's chances of finding a job as challenging and financially rewarding as the previous one are very slim. After age 50, it's nearly impossible. At 50, men and women in America are discarded, and there is no government law or agency to protect them. The Age Discrimination in Employment Act of 1967, which was supposed to protect against age discrimination in hiring, discharge, pay, promotions and fringe benefits, has been gutted by the courts. The Equal Employment Opportunity Commission has become a toothless old lion, and is unable to fend for the people it was created to protect.

American labor unions are confrontational for good reason. They are fighting for the very lives of their members. Union members are up against slave masters, not co-workers. Since the unions have no assurance that their workers' jobs are secure, they have no alternative but to fight for the highest wages they can get. Like a squirrel in summer, they must gather all they can in preparation for the long winter ahead, when they will be out on the streets.

A corporation's function is not to make millionaires of its executives. "Golden handcuffs" and "golden parachutes" are greed-motivated insurance policies that protect senior managers at the expense of the workers. Stock options and performance bonuses that are limited to executives are discriminatory against the mass of workers who also contribute to the company's success. These executive pay and protection plans ought to be against the law, and would be if America had even one Congressperson with some guts to stand up for what's right and make an issue of it.

A free and democratic country should guarantee an income to anyone who is willing to work. If this principle requires that the government be the employer of last resort, then the government ought to be prepared to take on this task. There are thousands of bridges and federal highways that need constant maintenance and day care services that need to be organized and staffed. There are miles of city sidewalks that are crumbling underfoot and public transportation systems that need repair. America's city streets are filthy, and toxic waste festers in abandoned lots and factories. There is no good reason for anybody to be out of work in the United States. The government is ignoring the peoples' needs.

The great disparity between the wealthy and poor in the U.S. must be addressed. When corporate executives earn millions of dollars per year, when a baseball player can command five million dollars a year—Bobby Bonilla is to make 29 million dollars over the next five years—when a rock star can demand five million dollars simply to make a TV commercial, while thousands of other Americans are homeless and living in the streets, then something has gone wrong.

Belief in the doctrine of the "economic man" is important to maintaining a healthy capitalist society. This "economic man" works hard and seizes opportunities to further his or her career and live a more comfortable life. America does not want to discourage people from going the extra mile. No country ever advances without that kind of participation by its citizens. But no one needs a "rapacious man" economy.

In some ways Japan is no better than the U.S. in protecting the rights of workers. Women, for example, did not even have the right to vote in Japan until 1947. Many women, in fact, still follow the old Confucian tradition of obedience to the male members of their family. Even today, the *okusan*, or wife, is supposed to stay inside the house. The women who do land positions in business often work too hard to have time to care for their children, and are rarely considered for advanced management positions.

The attitude of Japanese men to women outside the home is often degrading and sexist. Women are treated as sex objects to an extreme never reached in the United States. Even adult comic books, very popular in Japan, now feature a new hit character: "Rapeman."

The Boy's Festival is a national holiday, but the corresponding Girl's Festival is barely recognized. Almost 50 percent of all Japanese women are married according to arranged contractual agreements. One opposition political party, the Socialists, had a woman leader, Takako Doi. But she didn't really count in the overall scheme of things. Doi and her party are financed by Shin Kanemaru, a vice president of the Liberal Democratic Party and by a few of his conservative friends. Doi filled a window-dressing role for the nation, and made the Japanese look progressive to the West.

Cultural differences are not always human rights problems. People are oppressed only if they feel oppressed. For this reason, it is pointless to criticize Japan for its treatment of women and its minorities. The Japanese share few Western values, and they don't think they have a problem. There is no active women's movement in Japan. The *Burakumin* have an association, but it is largely mute. Even the Koreans are strangely silent, and they are probably the most disadvantaged of all.

These, however, are surface problems in international relations, and they can be ignored as long as the basic trade and political policies are fair. Peace with Japan is possible. Americans just have to recognize that their needs will have to be fought for at the negotiating tables, using all the trade weapons available. At home, if corporations in the U.S. and elsewhere want to be competitive in the world market-place, they must earn the support and loyalty of their employees. It is a foolish manager who neglects labor's contribution to production and profits. Labor is every bit as important as capital, and deserves the same consideration. An important corollary to this is the fact that no manager is worth an annual income measured in millions of dollars. The United States gets cut deeply on the issue of human rights. Americans need to address this issue quickly if they hope to compete with the rest of the world, much less the Japanese.

CHAPTER TEN

IIE: Japan Can Say No

"The physical and geographical circumstances of the two countries [USA & Japan] are totally different, to say nothing of their histories or their customs and manners. Your country [USA] is compact, (not scattered islands) though vast in area; it is peopled rather sparsely, though the total population is great; and it is immeasurably rich in natural resources. In fact, America is almost entirely self-sufficient and self-supporting. Ours is a country consisting of many small scattered islands, extremely overcrowded, and so poor in natural resources that we must largely depend on imports for our supply of raw materials. The neighbors with whom you may have troubles are either small or militarily quite impotent. On the contrary, we are face to face with two great continental Powers—China...and the Soviet Union...

"When you know this historical background and understand this overflowing vitality of our race you will see the impossibility of compelling us to stay still within the confines of our little island home. We are destined to grow and expand overseas."[1]

The above was written by Baron Reijiro Wakatsuki in 1935. Baron Wakatsuki was the Prime Minister of Japan on September 18, 1931, when the Japanese army blew up a train in China, killing several Japanese civilians. This act was blamed on the rag-tag Chinese militia and became known as the

Manchurian Incident. It was the rationale for Japan's annexation of Manchuria and the start of its China conquest.

Sixty years ago the world was faced with a growing Japanese military power. The Japanese occupied Taiwan, then known as Formosa, Korea and the bulk of Eastern China. Since the Second World War, Japan has concentrated on rebuilding its industrial base both at home and at strategic outposts around the world. The military structure has been reestablished only in outline form at this time, but it is beginning to develop some muscles. This will be discussed in the next chapter in greater detail, when we delve into Japan's plans for an aerospace industry.

In terms of historical imperatives (or those forces that compel nations to behave as they do) it helps to be aware of the conditions that were used to justify actions in the past. In 1935, when its population was 90 million people, Japan was already overcrowded. Today, it has 123 million people living in a mountainous, largely uninhabitable country that is roughly the size of Montana or California. Japan still has almost no domestic raw materials and is still faced with two continental powers across a narrow sea. But China and Russia are no more a threat to Japan today than they were in 1935. Neither country has demonstrated any recent interest in acquiring Japanese territory.

The pattern of relations between Japan and America since World War II reflects a growing Japanese defensiveness and an increasing American irritability reminiscent of the immediate pre-War period. Tyler Dennet, a pre-War Pulitizer Prize-winning history professor at Johns Hopkins University, wrote in 1941: "Hitherto Japan has never lacked for reputable advocates before the bar of American public opinion...The actual threats against Japanese security have been economic, not military. Since 1905 there has been no danger that any power would undertake to invade Japan as Western Europe has so often been fought over."[2] Of course, that picture changed after the Japanese attacked Pearl Harbor. However, since World War II, Dennet's statement is again true. Japan has no natural enemies.

Given this background, it is not surprising that the Japanese are again beginning to flex their muscles and advance their cause in world diplomacy, especially in Asia. Not long ago Japan offered to mediate the dispute in Cambodia, their first big venture into world politics since World War II. Then Japan announced that in 1989 Asia had become as big a trading region for it as the United States was. In effect, the Japanese are saying, they can get along without the United States.

The Japanese economy, though a miracle of modern times, is nonetheless most comparable to a circus highwire act. To work, it must be brazen and fearless. There is no net below the performers to catch them if they fall. One hundred twenty-three million people cannot revert to farming if their trading business fails them. The entire "act" is built on ocean shipping. With 70 percent of Japan's energy needs met by imported oil, a naval embargo of Persian Gulf oil would be devastating. Even the recent partial embargo—which stopped the shipment of only Iraqi and Kuwaiti oil—hurt them. In fact, the only way to move raw materials into Japan, and manufactured goods out, is by sea, so any restriction of the free movement of their ships is detrimental to Japanese interests.

Japan's economy relies on the sufferance and goodwill of its trading partners. Japan is a commercial nation that depends on world trade for its survival. It has the world's largest fleet of commercial ships, not counting flags of convenience.[3] Take away the ships or the sea lanes, and Japan fails as a nation. Without a great power navy, or a nuclear strike capability, Japan must rely—for now—only on commercial travelers: A nation of salesmen dependent on the satisfaction of its customers.[4]

The American Navy has been guaranteeing Japan's cargo ships' safety at sea for the past 47 years. It has shouldered an enormous financial burden that has helped to cripple the American economy and allowed Japan to concentrate on building its trade. In return, American recompensation has recently risen to a paltry 40 percent of the expenses of keeping U.S. troops in Japan. It seems that America has spent its scarce resources keeping the world safe—for Japanese shipping.

However, despite its lack of great military power, Japan is an economic empire that can easily threaten and manipulate the economy of many other nations. Why does Japan need a navy if it has that kind of power without one? The fact is that the nature of warfare has changed since World War II. Nuclear weapons have made traditional combat between world powers mostly obsolete. Navies are needed now only to protect against smaller nations like Iraq that cause regional disruptions of trade. What has happened is that trade has now become the modern way to wage war. The goals of war are still the same, though: Economic growth and territorial aggrandizement.

In fact, those nations that most successfully control manufacturing and trade will, in the future, own the world and reap the benefits that wealth bestows. The Japanese have no need of a navy to conquer Hawaii when they already own 60 percent of the islands' land. They have no need of an army to conquer Siberia or Manchuria anymore.

It is highly unlikely that the United States will ever threaten Japan with military invasion. It is equally unlikely that Japan will ever become a world military power; it is far too costly. But it would be foolish to suppose that Japan will not again become a great Asian power. The Japanese are already well on their way to achieving that position. And, in spite of Japan's constitutional prohibitions against military involvement, the government regularly tests the nation's willingness to involve its troops overseas: It did its best to drum up support for sending rear echelon troops to the Persian Gulf War and forces to support the United Nations in the Middle East. So much for the constitution: In Japan it can be interpreted in any way that's convenient. To date, the Diet has not considered it convenient, and no troops have been sent out of Japan.

What is daily becoming most likely, given Japan's obvious plans for developing a future space rocket launching operation, is a nuclear deterent capability. Japan will almost certainly arm itself with nuclear missiles beginning sometime around the turn of the century. It's not that these missiles would be used to attack the United States, or even the Asian mainland, for that matter. Japan knows that in a major war it would be destroyed. But what it does have within its power is blackmail. How many American Congresspeople would risk Japanese nuclear retaliation to save the Korean peninsula from a Japanese-occupation force?

It is far better to consider the possibilities now than to be surprised by the realities later. The Japanese should be content to dominate the world economically, but as the United States and what was the Soviet Union reduce their nuclear arms, Japan's military power becomes more significant.

World economic power already resides in Tokyo, and when viewed from the United States the future only looks bleaker. Japan is winning this economic war by destroying the West's manufacturing base. Soon the United States, the former Soviet Union, most of Europe and the British Commonwealth nations will be unable to afford to maintain their nuclear and other military systems.

The annual budget deficits in the United States already stretch beyond the imagination. George Bush's budget request for Fiscal Year 1992 was 1.45 trillion dollars! That was over 25 percent of gross national product. In Reagan's final year the budget represented 22.3 percent of GNP.[5] This is a far faster boom in spending in two years than the Carter Administration managed in four years.

Anybody with a third grade education knows that someday the piper will have to be paid. When today's warheads are obsolete, and plutonium is too expensive to produce; when the rocket fuel is too old to be reliable, and the ships' engines are cracking; when supercomputers and high-density semiconductors are Japanese exclusives, then the West will have lost the war.

In the United States, Americans are living on their patrimony. Factories are deteriorating rapidly and are not being replaced at anywhere near the rate needed to secure a future for the next generation. In 1989, Japan, with only half of the United States' population, became the world's biggest spender on new factories and equipment. The Washington-based Council of Competitiveness, an organization of university professors, union officials and corporate executives, reported that in 1989 Japan spent 36 billion dollars more on capital investments than did the United States: 549 billion dollars vs. 513 billion dollars. "This marks the first time that any country has out-invested the United States in plant and equipment in absolute terms since World War II," the study reported.

In 1990 Japan spent 586 billion dollars on new factories and equipment, compared with 524 billion dollars by the United States.[6]

For the Japanese, saying no to somebody is considered bad manners. So, when they don't agree, they usually try to say maybe or probably, or try to avoid the issue entirely. However, the Japanese are finding that in the West saying no is not only acceptable, but desirable when a negative response is the most honest answer.

Japanese businessmen have been learning this lesson over the years, and now are encouraging their government to learn the lesson as well.

In Morita's book, he tells us that during the Reagan Administration, Japan was forced to limit its automobile exports to the United States to two million cars per year. Publicly it was called a "voluntary restraint agreement." When the American economy improved, and the Big Three auto makers in Detroit had made some production deals in Japan, the quota was then increased. The American automobile manufacturers made huge profits by importing Japanese-made cars under Detroit brand names. However, the Japanese brand name automobiles suffered a temporary loss of market share in the process. This was a case, says Morita, where the Japanese Prime Minister and the Ministry of International Trade and Industry should have said no to America. Japan didn't need Detroit to help them sell cars in the United States.

Morita thinks that this was an unfair trade practice, and that the Japanese government should have said so. The Big Three auto makers increased their profits enormously at Japan's expense. Individuals such as Lee Iacocca at Chrysler and Roger Smith at General Motors received more than a million dollars each in bonuses as a result. This amounted to special treatment for the American manufacturers, says Morita. Japan should have told the United States and the Big Three that they were being hypocritical by criticizing others for being unfair and then ripping off the Japanese at the first opportunity.

It's hard to argue with this assertion. It's a mystery why Detroit continues to buy Japanese automobiles and parts when, for the sake of some short-term profits, it is just cutting its own throat. Japan doesn't like giving up business, but understands that in the long-run Detroit's shortsighted policy will drive America out of the automobile business. In the future, though, Japan will probably be more and more reluctant to give up even the short-term profits. As Japan grows stronger, there is less need to cater to the United States.

The concern among many people in the West is that with its sudden wealth, Japan may now revert to its arrogant nationalism of the 1930s. There are signs that Japan's aging leadership is trying to bequeath its power to its sons in defiance of Japan's constitutional demand for a meritocracy. Power is often hidden from view in Japan, and this can be confusing to Westerners. The West assumes that the Prime Minister of Japan runs the government. Yet in reality, professional bureaucrats in various ministries often have the final word.

Shin Kanemaru, a behind-the-scenes-power broker, went to North Korea and made promises of Japanese aid in the spirit of political reconciliation. His action annoyed some members of the government, but Kanemaru's promises became policy. Kanemaru's base of power is the telecommunications industry, and it has given him the power to effectively appoint and influence previous prime ministers, including Nakasone and Kaifu. This power, both bureaucratic and industry-based, is much easier to keep within the ruling families and much harder for governments to regulate than it is in the United States. This influence also runs parallel with Japanese history since it marks a return to hereditary power bases.

Young people in Japan, free of any wartime memories or struggles with poverty, are developing some troubling attitudes. In a 1990 *Wall Street Journal* poll, 25 percent of the respondents under age 30 thought that in the event of a future war, the enemy would be the United States. For those under age 20 the percentage rises to 30 percent.[7] Twenty-three percent thought the ex-Soviet Union would be the future enemy.

Masahiko Ishizuka, an editorial writer for Tokyo's newspaper, *Nihon Keizai Shimbun*, was quoted as saying, "The ratio of lazy persons is much higher in the U.S. We have a longer history than the U.S.A. We should be proud of our own culture. We must export our culture."[8] In January 1992, Japan's new Prime Minister Kiichi Miyazawa echoed this charge of American laziness saying that America had lost its work ethic.

These attitudes represent a burgeoning nationalism and an intolerance of things foreign. There is a barely suppressed rage that seems to be bubbling beneath the surface of many Japanese people, especially teenagers and young adults.

Morita tends to see the world in simplistic terms. "Timing," he says, "is crucial when negotiations are in progress. Unless Japan learns to say no at the right moment, the Americans take the situation for granted and later insist that there was no opposition when the demands were made. That is the American way. They take advantage of Japanese courtesy to get their own demands met."[9] It's difficult for Americans to deal openly with people who do not always speak what's on their mind.

Sometimes, however, the reverse occurs: A Japanese diplomat will say exactly what he doesn't really believe. For example, when the Japanese Prime Minister comes to Washington and agrees to open up Japan's home markets to U.S. business, he smiles a lot, shakes hands all around, and then goes back to Tokyo and forgets the whole nasty episode. When U.S. Congresspeople later ask for a progress report, they are amazed to find that nothing has been done.

The Japanese point of view, however, is that the U.S. government fails to recognize the changes that have occurred in the last ten to 15 years in its trade relations with Japan. The United States has gone from complementary trade with Japan to competitive trade and now to dependent trade. It needs Japan today as it has never needed Japan before. But because of its cultural prohibitions, Japan is finding it increasingly difficult to tell the West that complaints about the trade imbalance are misdirected. America should be looking to itself to correct its own lack of savings, investment and product development.

For the most part, the United States imports products from Japan that require high-tech production expertise. The days of importing silk and dolls are long gone. Many of these new products are for military purposes, but the private sector, too, is requiring more and more sophisticated Japanese technology. In some cases, even relatively simple products, such as small appliances, are in demand because Japan's production process has become so mechanically efficient. In return, Japan uses the United States as a raw materials source, and imports those few products which it has not yet begun to manufacture domestically.

Japan's insecurity stems from its age-old problems: The more and more crowded living conditions caused by an oppressive population density; the continued flow of people from the rural land to cities with inadequate housing; the consequent growing dependence on the factory for employment; the high prices; the large production surpluses that must be exported because they are not absorbed domestically; the growing trade protectionist sentiment among Japan's trading partners; the reluctance of prosperous countries to allow tariff-free importation of Japanese products; and the exclusion of Japanese immigrants from other industrialized countries.

Morita tells a revealing story in his book that cuts to the heart of the problem of negotiating with the Japanese. Namely, Japanese children do not learn how to quarrel or fight in the same way that Western children do. Their culture requires a bending of the personal will to the higher will of the group, the company, or the manager. So the Japanese become accustomed to saying yes. They tend to hope that other people will eventually see how unhappy they are simply by being near them, *ishin denshin*, and then stop bothering them without having to be asked. In the worst of times, the Japanese remain hopeful that they will eventually be understood even if they cannot verbalize their complaints. Morita, however, says that this is foolish thinking outside of Japan. Wordless telepathy doesn't work in the West. "Japan," he says, "must learn to speak and to say no to outrageous demands. If we do not learn to do this, Japan will become even more isolated in this interdependent world."[10]

CHAPTER ELEVEN

HARA: A Centralized Force

On July 28, 1990, at a conference in Jakarta, the Malaysian Foreign Minister warned his Asian colleagues that Japan could replace the Soviet Union as Asia's most worrisome military threat. Taro Nakayama, Japan's Foreign Minister, replied that Japan would not use force against its neighbors.

But after Japan's brutal military hegemony in Asia during the first half of this century, perhaps it's not unreasonable for the other Asian nations to fear their resurgent island neighbor. When these countries look at Japan's military budget, and see that Japan has become the third-largest military spender in the world, they ask about the need for these expenditures.[1] Where is the enemy, they wonder. Where is the threat to Japan that justifies this spending?

According to the Self-Defense Agency, Japan spent 41.3 billion dollars on its military in the fiscal year ended March 1991. This compared with 103 billion dollars for the Soviet Union and 313.9 billion dollars for the United States.[2] Even considering that the cost of armaments is high in Japan, these expenditures put Japan ahead of West Germany, the United Kingdom and France. Japan also has a five-year budget for procurements, not including maintenance of forces, of 156 billion dollars which makes its the fastest growing military budget in the industrialized world. It has been growing at a fairly steady five percent a year for more than a decade.[3]

Ishihara tells the West that for twenty years he has been calling America's defense of Japan a sham. He denies that Japan has had a free ride on the defense issue. "The U.S. nuclear umbrella is an illusion."[4] Without Japan's high technology there would not have been an intercontinental ballistic missile deterent.

Ishihara believes that an increased Japanese defense capability, one that exploits its technology to the maximum, is worthwhile. Whatever Japan's future military relations with the United States may be, he calls for a reorganization of Japanese military forces. He suggests that Japan consider extending the defense of Pacific sea-lanes up to 1,000 miles from home. "We should develop the most persuasive and demonstrable deterrent formula which would, without any doubt, show our adversaries that any attack on Japan will end with unbearable damage to the aggressor from both a strategic and a tactical viewpoint."[5]

Seldom in history has such a flagrant warning been issued to the world. Ishihara, who represents a significant portion of Japan's conservative politicians, is telling the West in no uncertain terms that Japan must develop a strategic deterrent force, that is, intercontinental ballistic missiles with nuclear warheards. If Japan's true purpose is defense, the only possible adversaries that ICBMs could be used against are the United States and Russia. If not, then China, India and probably Pakistan, all possessors of atomic weapons, need to be concerned.

"The time has come for Japan to tell the United States that we do not need American protection."[6] Ishihara is demanding that his people reject any American support, yet at the same time he realizes that such a change cannot take place without a national consensus which does not yet exist. Still, he says, "financially and technologically, there are no barriers to accomplishing this goal in the near future."[7]

"Count on this," wrote A.M. Rosenthal in a column. "The Japanese Army will soon again become a political force at home, a constant threat to the delicate, complex civilian equilibrium that is now the base and protection of Japan's democratic society."[8]

The good news is that the Japanese people seem to be unimpressed by their military. Before he left office Prime Minister Toshiki Kaifu asked the director of the defense agency, Yozo Ishikawa, to reassess the Soviet threat. He felt that perhaps the military budget could be cut due to the change in Soviet political developments. Then, after the successful visit of Eduard Shevardnadze, then Soviet Foreign Minister, to Tokyo in September 1990, the announcement was made that Japan no longer saw the Soviet Union as a military threat. This was a diplomatic move designed to restore normal relations and to reach a peace settlement that has eluded the two countries since the end of World War II. However, Mikhail Gorbachev's visit to Japan in April 1991 did not settle the issue of the Kurile Islands and other obstacles to a permanent peace treaty. Consequently, there has been no significant move to reduce Japanese military spending.

In September 1992, President Boris N. Yeltsin of Russia plans to visit Tokyo. With German Foreign Minister Hans-Dietrich Genscher's mediation, Russia is finally expected to return the Kurile Islands in exchange for massive Japanese aid. It remains to be seen if an agreement will have any affect on Japanese military spending.

The military school at Etajima, complains academy superintendent Rear Admiral Yasuaki Imaizumi, graduates 425 officer candidates each year, but loses about 15 percent of them to private business. It's hard to recruit professional military people to create an officer corps. People are too interested in civilian careers. The country authorizes a military force of 240,000 people and bases most of them on Hokkaido, the island closest to Russia, where they do not call attention to themselves as they would in the more densely populated main islands. Japan does not have a conscription system, and its navy is often short of sailors.

The Japanese people seem to support the idea of a military force as long as they do not have to serve personally, and as long as it does not assume a high profile. They don't really trust their military people. They seem to understand that if the military gains ascendancy in the country, Japan may again be forced to follow the military's program. As a result, the people want their uniformed forces kept on a short leash.

The Japanese government, however, is beginning to talk about sharing peacekeeping responsibilities in the Pacific with the United States. This talk of additional military responsibility worries many older people in Japan who remember the Pacific War, as it is known in Japan, but seems to have a favorable audience among the younger generation. In the early days of the Persian Gulf crisis, Japan was severely criticized by many governments for not offering its military forces to help enforce the embargo. This criticism hurt Japanese pride, and left them wondering what their role in the crisis should be. Eventually Prime Minister Toshiki Kaifu caved in, notwithstanding Japan's constitution, and requested that service troops be sent to help the effort. However, none were sent.

This ambivalence about the military slows Japan's response rates in emergencies. The Japanese want very much to be a world power again, but at the same time many remember what an aggressive military stance led to fifty years ago. It would be a major change in the strategic balance of forces in Asia if Japan did decide to take on full military partnership with the

U.S.A. Psychologically, the Japanese people have not yet made that adjustment.

Given these circumstances, it is puzzling why the United States government is pressing for Japanese rearmament. Why should Japan have a force of ultramodern FSX fighter planes, a developing missile capability, and a growing fleet of LSTs? Article nine of the MacArthur Constitution, which prohibited the imposition of land, sea or air forces on the Japanese people, has been openly flouted with U.S. government encouragement. Relying on the good sense of the Japanese people to control their burgeoning military capability is not only futile, but dangerous. In the end, the people of Japan are malleable. They will bend with the wind and do as they are told. They always have.

Consider that 90 percent of Japan's top bureaucrats are graduates of the University of Tokyo's Law School. Democracy in Japan means rule by clique, and everybody is a member of a clique. These special interest groups, clubs, *keiretsus*, corporations and *dojos* exist to form a consensus. Leadership of a Japanese clique is a powerful position, because the members are loyal to a degree unknown in the West. The group is molded by its leader, the *sensei*, and the members pay him enormous respect and fealty. In addition, these leaders are often members of regional or national organizations which have ties to the powers in Tokyo or Osaka.

The people of Japan are pollen; the group is the flower, the whole. When the *Kamikaze*, or wind spirit, blows its breath of change across the land, the flowers spill their pollen, and the people are transported to where they are wanted. The redeification of the emperor in October 1991 was important because it reestablished the traditional links in *bushido*. It restored the spiritual imperative that leads the Japanese in unison.

This description of the Japanese power structure may lead you to believe that it resembles a pyramid with a pointed top. Nothing could be further from the truth. Instead of a pointed top to this pyramid, there is more of a mesa effect, that is, no central power or core of influence in Japan. One of the more frustrating things about dealing with the Japanese is that power centers do exist, but they are shifting phenomena like the wind, real but hard to put your finger on. Karel van Wolferen calls it the "elusive Japanese state. The Japanese state vanishes once one considers the question of accountability."9

Dissent also exists in Japan, but it must find circuitous routes of expression. People do not routinely stand up and confront their group's leadership. According to an ancient Japanese proverb, the nail that sticks up is hammered down.

When Prime Minister Toshiki Kaifu asked the Diet to send Japanese troops to the Persian Gulf in a non-combatant role, he was not only defeated, but subjected to a great deal of vilification from both the opposition political parties and Tokyo's university students. Kaifu was ousted later in 1991 by his own party in spite of the fact that L.D.P. insiders had probably put him up to it.

The real powers in Japan, at least in part identifiable as Shin Kanemaru, an important financial backer of the L.D.P., and the members of the Federation of Economic Organizations, known as the *Keidanren*, do not want to waste Japanese resources on unplanned, inappropriate and inopportune military expenditures. However, it was necessary to address the United States demands for greater Japanese participation in the Gulf. So, Kaifu was allowed to propose the help, but was soundly defeated by his own Liberal Democratic Party and by the Socialists. Eventually, the Japanese were pressured by the United States into a financial contribution to the war effort and donated 13 billion dollars.

However, in spite of Japan's current reluctance to commit itself militarily overseas, the build-up of its armed forces continues rapidly at home. The self-defense forces have grown to impressive levels:[10]

Total armed forces	240,000
Tanks	1,200
Artillery	830
Combat aircraft	424
Armed helicopters	48

An examination of Japanese naval strengths, and their changes over the past dozen years, does reveal some shifts in emphasis from purely home waters protection to a greater ability for extended cruises. The addition of fuel tankers to the fleet is one manifestation of this shift. (See chart below). The growth of the larger destroyer class over the frigate class, as well as the disappearance of corvettes, also suggests a shift to a more offensive posture. The build-up in landing craft is also hard to justify for purely defensive purposes even allowing for the fact that Japan is an island chain. However, on balance, the following chart, drawn from *Jane's Fighting Ships* of 1980-1981 and 1991-1992, indicates that Japan's navy is still essentially a defensive force.

The figures below do not take account of the Japanese Maritime Safety Agency, which is comparable to the United States Coast Guard. This branch of the military has a fleet of 440 naval craft, of which 46 would count as frigates or corvettes in most of the world's navies.[11] Ships and submarines are held in the Japanese navy only 16 years, far short of their useful lives, and then are reassigned either to the M.S.A. or as training vessels. Thus, while the ships are not counted as part of the navy, they are still available to the country. Japan maintains an active ship and submarine building program so that for the foreseeable future, it will have a very modern navy. The latest destroyers under construction will have AEGIS missile capability, which is too expensive for any of the European navies.

CHANGES IN JAPANESE NAVAL STRENGTH

FLEET	1979	1990
Submarines, Patrol, Diesel	13	15
Destroyers	33	43
Frigates	15	18
Corvettes	11	0
Torpedo boats	5	4
Patrol, Coastal	6	9
LSTs*	6	6
LSUs*	0	2
Landing Craft*	0	44
Minesweepers, Coastal	31	32
Tenders	n.a.	16
Fuel tankers	0	37

FLEET AIR ARM

FLEET	1979	1990
Air ASW Sqdns (Anti-Submarine)	14	16
Air Training Squadrons	4	6
Air Transport Sqdn	1	1
MCM Squadron	1	1

* Amphibious landing forces for troops, tanks and equipment.

A chart of the evolution of Japan's merchant marine presents a curious picture. Over the past 12 years Japan has dramatically reduced the gross tonnage carried under its flag, but has maintained the number of ships at sea. Economically, this doesn't add up. In one sense the disparity simply reflects the over-capacity in the ocean carrier industry, and the Japanese may simply have shifted to smaller, newer vessels. But why not fewer and larger ships if economy is the goal? This shift does have one important military advantage: The Japanese are continuing to train a lot of potential naval officers and men at sea, even with the reduced tonnage.

MERCHANT MARINE

FLEET	1979	1990
Vessels	9,981	10,000
Gross tons	39,992,925	27,077,943

The word *hara*, used in Japanese martial arts, refers to the concentration of mind and force that is often needed to prevail in a contest. A good example is the archer who plants his feet squarely, draws the string slowly to his chin, controls his breathing and mentally directs the arrow to its target at that one critical moment when he releases the tension on the string. That's *hara*, and it is a term carried over into politics and trade relations as well.

It is important to understand the thinking of the people masterminding many of the major changes in Japan. They are the dominant, reactionary forces within the Liberal Democratic Party who want to see Japan retake its position of dominance in Asia. By examining them, we can see *hara* at work.

Writing in the 1990 summer issue of *Foreign Affairs*, Fred Ikle, under Secretary of Defense for Policy in the Reagan Administration, and Terumasa Nakanishi of the Research Institute for Peace and Security (Tokyo), said, "It seems unlikely that Japan's body politic would remain content through the end of this decade to see the nation a mere bystander on matters that affect the strategic order of the world." It should come as no surprise to anybody, especially the countries of Southeast Asia, that Japan is planning on dominating the "Pacific Era."

Ishihara, in the original Japanese version of his book, urged his compatriots to learn what it is that makes Japan strong, and then to project that strength in their dealings with the West.

Ishihara says, for example, that American politicians told him there is a new power shift in the world that made the United States and the then-Soviet Union allies instead of enemies. He was expected to believe that this development should somehow scare Japan. "These same politicians," he reports, "indicated that since both the Americans and the Soviets are white, at a final confrontation, they might gang up on a non-white Japan." In the official translation, this was moderated to "leaving Japan out in the cold." In either case, it would have been helpful if he had given us the names of these U.S. politicians, but it does reflect a typical attitude of the ultra-right wing of the Liberal Democratic Party in Japan. Something else to remember is that the L.D.P. is neither liberal nor democratic, and it is the only party that runs the country.

Ishihara may be being provocative for his own purposes. Whatever the case, he has reaped the benefits of being a fanatical nationalist. His book became a bestseller in Japan, and so did the follow-up book, *Still The Japan That Can Say No*. This indicates that Ishihara is finding some sympathetic support for his belligerent ideas among the Japanese people.

"Japan has substantial national strength to deal with other nations, yet some of the powerful cards it holds have been wasted diplomatically," says Ishihara, angry with the United States and with his own foreign service people. Japan will not waste its diplomatic high cards in the future he is warning. Trade agreements will become more difficult to reach.

Ishihara condemns the United States Congress as being "too hysterical to trust." He argues that it was unfair to pass a resolution telling Japan that it cannot sell to Russia because it violates the Japanese license to manufacture these high-tech products. He believes that if Japan goes to the trouble of making something, it automatically has the right to sell the product to any country it wants to—even to America's potential enemies. A license to manufacture should not interfere with Japan's marketing program.

The question here is not whether or not Japan has the right to sell the products it manufactures, but just how thoroughly committed it is to its alliance with other Western nations. Will it stand by them in the event of a boycott against the enemies of the West? The answer is obviously no.

Kentaro Aikawa, President of Mitsubishi Heavy Industries, also sees some U.S. business concerns as unwarranted. In his case, he has tried to calm American fears that his company is preparing to launch a massive development campaign in aerospace and commercial aviation. "There will never be the day when the Japanese aircraft industry will catch up with the American aircraft industry," he told *The New York Times*.[12]

This scenario is all so familiar it is hard to believe that the Japanese keep expecting the United States to buy such assurances. The process begins with the licensing of American or European technology that allows the Japanese to get started in the business. This has happened with steel, automobiles, consumer electronics, semiconductors and machine tools. Then, as soon as the business gets on its feet, the Japanese company conveniently forgets the original agreement that the technology and the products associated with it are supposed to be confined to allied Western countries.

Moreover, regardless of how important the product is to the military security of the United States, Japan feels free to sell whatever it manufactures. For Japan, broadening the marketing base is essential to improving its manufacturing efficiency. Japan is baffled by American Congresspeople's inability to understand this simple fact. How else could Japanese industry grow and dominate its competitors?

The conflict between Mitsubishi and U.S. aircraft business is a good example of the friction between Japanese business and the U.S. Congress. At the Mitsubishi plant in Nagoya, there lies row upon row of F-15 fighters, Boeing 767 fuselages and Japanese rockets all being constructed in the same place. Faced with this growing Japanese capability in aircraft manufacturing, the U.S. Congress was right to be concerned about Japanese participation in the FSX fighter project. Given the history of Japanese reliability as partners, it was appropriate to ask if Mitsubishi could be trusted.

The FSX fighter is the newest, most sophisticated airplane on the drawing boards. It is light years ahead of the planes now in service, and there has been a lot of concern about sharing this technology.

Mitsubishi is Japan's leading aircraft producer, and if allowed the high level of participation in the FSX project that it wanted, Mitsubishi would have quickly learned all the lessons of aircraft system integration that it has taken the United States years to develop. It would have given the Japanese a great boost in developing their own military production capabilities and their own commercial aviation industry. The questions U.S. Congresspeople faced were: Why help Japan overtake yet another American industry? And, why risk Japan's selling our aviation technology to unfriendly countries?

Interestingly, even though the FSX model agreed upon for joint development is a design derivative of General Dynamics' F-16, Ishihara suggests that it is based on a Mitsubishi development. And, indeed, if they produce the plane he describes, it may well be a Japanese development. Ishihara claims that a contemporary of his, the chief engineer at Mitsubishi, designed the FSX fighter. (His claim is reminiscent of the hardliners in the old Soviet Union, who gave the U.S.S.R. credit for inventing everything from planes to television.) But in all probability, what this really means is that already we are seeing the political groundwork being laid to attempt to justify the sale of FSX technology to Japan's future customers, whoever they be.

This Mitsubishi engineer is also said to have told Ishihara that "Japan should have its own capacity to provide such equipment." Ishihara thinks that this notion astonishes Americans. He doesn't give the West a lot of credit for either brains or for past contributions to the Japanese defense industry. That the Japanese want to have aircraft capability to provide for their own defense is perfectly understandable. However, because of the small volumes of warplanes manufactured in Japan, they will cost from 30 percent to 100 percent more per plane than they would if bought directly from the United States. Why, then, does Japan's need for self-sufficiency extend to military aircraft?

Under no system of government or economy does this kind of procurement program make sense. However, in light of Mitsubishi's effort to negotiate for a Boeing 777 production partnership it begins to make some sense. The highest technology is used in the military FSX fighter plane, and Japan has now been granted sufficient production participation in that program to quickly master the systems integration of airplane manufacturing. In other words, the high price Mitsubishi is paying to produce the FSX in Japan will be considered a production development expense so that the company can also learn to make big civilian airliners, such as the Boeing 777 (known as the 767-X while in the development stage).

After the Japanese won the important battle with the U.S. Congress over their rights to the FSX, Mitsubishi would have been happy to have received any part of the Boeing 777 contract. As it turns out, Mitsubishi will be building at least 20 percent of the new airliner without having to invest the one billion dollars that Boeing initially wanted from them for a 25 percent production share. With such new technology and methods now available, Mitsubishi will be in position to challenge the entire U.S. aerospace industry for marketing dominance by the end of the 1990s.

There is not much that can be done to curb the foolishness of executives such as Lawrence Clarkson, Boeing's senior vice president of government and international affairs. Clarkson told *The Wall Street Journal* that Japanese participation in the Boeing 777 project would be "a step up from what they're doing on the 767, but not a big step."[13] He's apparently not at all worried that Japan could use the knowledge of Boeing technology to build its own aerospace industry. Technology is inevitably "a fleeting thing," Clarkson says. With this attitude, it certainly is.

Fortunately, there are still a few voices of sanity to be heard at the Commerce Department. One of the former senior officials there, Clyde Prestowitz Jr., was quoted as saying, "Boeing is either being arrogant, ignorant or just blowing smoke. Aerospace, is probably Japan's single most important target."[14]

Ishihara raves about the FSX fighter capabilities. "The FSX is a marvelous and formidable fighter. No existing fighter, including the F-15 or the F-16, can match it in a dog fight."[15] In fact, this warplane will be so extraordinary an advance in avionics that Casper Weinberger, the Reagan Administration's Secretary of Defense, wanted Japan kept out of this project entirely. However, in the end he was defeated in a controversial vote undoubtedly influenced by Japanese PAC money.

Casper Weinberger viewed the rise of Japanese militarism with some trepidation. He's not alone. Dr. Jean-Pierre Lehmann, director of InterMatrix Japan, a U.S.-, European- and Asian-based international business consulting firm, wrote in the March 1990 issue of *The World Paper*, a business magazine distributed mostly in Asia, that "A robust Japanese defense industry emerging in the '90s appears inevitable." The question is, why? Where is the enemy? And how will Japan's military hardware be used?

Unfortunately, Ishihara reports, Japan has not yet developed a powerful enough engine for its version of the FSX fighter plane. To its chagrin, Japan was facing the prospect of having to purchase the less powerful engines that come with the F-15 and F-16 fighters. This prospect left the Japanese military planners extremely unsatisfied. They thought that they could buy the more powerful engines they wanted in France, which has a very aggressive export policy for military equipment. But the French attitude put the Japanese off; they questioned French reliability. The Japanese thought it was hypocritical to sell armaments at the same time that country's President Mitterrand is advocating truces all over the world.

If France won't sell what the Japanese need, they might well go to the Russians, although the quality of the engines there is not up to par. The new FSX, equipped with Russian engines, would have only 95 percent of the speed of existing F-15 and F-16 planes, according to Ishihara. The Japanese must have already investigated this option of using Russian engines, and that admission should be registered solidly in the Pentagon's memory banks. It raises a further question about Japanese solidarity with Western allies. However, the point Ishihara is making is that there are a lot of places to go shopping.

As it turned out, the Japanese signed an agreement with their ex-ally Daimler-Benz A.G. of Germany. Mitsubishi will share in the technological data and be assured of first quality jet engines at reasonable prices.

Ishihara also reports on Japan's expectations from the Mitsubishi FSX fighter plane. He reveals that the Japanese version is designed to make a 360 degree turn in one-third of the space required for F-15 or F-16 planes: 1,600 meters vs. 5,000 meters. Air war, Ishihara says, can be compared to a game of tag, for maneuverability is more important than speed. Even if Japan had to give up five percentage points on speed the Japanese FSX would still have greater maneuverability, he claimed, before the deal with Daimler-Benz was signed.

"Mitsubishi's FSX fighter can get right on an enemy plane and send heat-seeking missiles with 100 percent accuracy," Ishihara reports.[16] According to *Jane's World Aircraft* of 1991-92, Japan's initial plans are to produce 170 of these aircraft between 1997 and 2001, a formidable force that will replace the 77 older F-1 fighter planes currently being used.

"The FSX was a surprise to the Americans," Ishihara says, "as were the Zero fighters in the Second World War. In those days, they never expected to see such an advanced fighter. It virtually controlled the air at the beginning of the war. We have shocked them again with the FSX," Ishihara is gloating.[17] He realizes that the United States does not want this plane produced outside of America beyond the sphere of its control. "The Japanese FSX is equipped with four vertical stabilizers similar to shark's fins. [If so, this is a significant design difference.] Each acts as a steering mechanism, like the steering wheel of a four wheel drive automobile that can make a complete turn in a small area without moving back and forth."[18] This gives it a turning responsiveness beyond anything else in the air. While the Japanese cannot claim credit for this innovation, it was Japanese engineers who developed it into a workable idea, Ishihara is proud to note.

"Russian fighters are also equipped with Japanese technology, especially in ceramics and carbon fibers," he brags. This, of course, is the heart of stealth technology making planes invisible to radar. It was supposed to be an American exclusive. With this admission, all thinking people in the West are left to wonder why the United States has bothered to spend billions of dollars on military stealth research only to hear some Japanese politician brag about how the benefit of that research has been delivered to the one power on earth that might have used it against the United States.

The new agreement for joint manufacturing of the FSX will allow Japan to produce just the plane it wants. When Yasuhiro Nakasone was Prime Minister of Japan, he came under fire from his party's right wing for giving General Dynamics too much control of the project. But in the final agreement, Japanese military minds prevailed. General Dynamics will build about 40 percent of a plane based on its F-16, while Mitsubishi will build just about everything, except the engines, for its own version of the FSX. The U.S. Congress should not be surprised when Japan ends up with the better airplane.

The deal between McDonnell Douglas and South Korea is also worthy of mention. In the summer of 1990, a three billion dollar agreement was reached to sell 120 F/A-18 fighters to the Seoul government. However, as a part of the package, Seoul wanted McDonnell Douglas to hand over some very sophisticated aviation technology so that it could manufacture the bulk of these units. Not surprisingly, this request came through almost immediately after the U.S. Congress balked at giving virtually the same information to the Japanese for the FSX project.

Senator Alan Dixon (D-Illinois) raised some serious questions about this deal with Korea, but Congressional approval was granted anyway. When Senator Dixon subsequently learned that a secret aide-mémoire had been made a part of the package by the White House, he introduced a bill to force President Bush to disclose the secret terms. The terms were classified Top Secret, and according to Senator Dixon's office, were never made public. However, the Koreans changed their minds after the controversy died down and decided to buy the F-16 instead with the same manufacturing rights. One can almost smell the collusion between the Japanese and their hired cohorts in Korea. Remember that the new FSX fighter is based on F-16 technology. Congress seems to have got side-tracked on the barter/offset issue, which was only a red herring in this discussion.

The Koreans have been accused in the past of improperly selling U.S. military hardware and technology to third countries, and if they need such sophisticated aircraft, they ought to come up with the cash. It makes no sense for them to manufacture part of this order, because their unit costs will be significantly higher than what McDonnell Douglas will charge for delivering the planes. The only purpose South Korea could have in wanting to manufacture airplanes is to become partners with Japan in the commercial aviation manufacturing business. There is still time for Congress to review and disapprove this treaty.

It's staggering to think that the Aerospace Industries Association, a lobbying group in Washington, D.C., can see the picture otherwise. Joel Johnson, one of its vice presidents, said, "there is nothing unusual or threatening about this sale. What would be more threatening is if we mess this up and they turn around and buy European aircraft instead." He claims that "Congressmen keep forgetting that we have current competitors."[19]

On the face of it, this is a compelling argument. But you only have to dig a little beneath the surface to realize that the Europeans don't have such sophisticated technology either. Nobody makes fighter jets or commercial aircraft as well as the Americans. The aerospace industry is the one area in which the United States is still ahead of the rest of the world. It may be a tenuous lead, but nonetheless Americans ought to be fighting very hard to hold on to it. The Koreans will not go to Europe for warplanes because the U.S. planes are far superior.

Another area of real concern to the United States is the Japanese approach to basic research. What research? The Japanese don't do basic research. They have the Western world to provide that service. Morita himself said that Japanese business innovations are in product development. The Japanese excel in taking somebody else's idea or product and refining it to make it better. That's how the Japanese will enter and then dominate the military and civilian aircraft industries. By the end of this decade that's how Japan will become a major force in the spaceship business. That's how Japan will develop an intercontinental missile force that could pose a military threat. The same rockets that launch a satellite can also launch a warhead.

Japan tries hard not to spend money on research that yields only knowledge. It is far too dangerous for them. Think what would happen if a Japanese researcher spent one million dollars and didn't discover something wonderful. The researcher would be shamed; he'd be so humiliated that he would be tempted to commit suicide. No, Japan needs a product that it can sell or that will enhance its national power as a reward for the research expenditure. And Japan needs to be able to see the results in advance. Decisions for research and development projects must be made in committee so that the risk can be shared. Such a set-up would not suit Western basic reseach in which personal initiative and daring are expected, even required.

Given this difference in research strategies, it is surprising to learn that four U.S. executive agencies and one Congressional committee recently went to Japan to solicit aid for basic research projects in the United States. Imagine the Japanese contributing one billion dollars to a supercollider project in Texas. Or supporting a multi-billion dollar effort to map the human genetic system. The whole Japanese Finance Ministry would first have to commit *seppuku* en masse.

Why should Japan spend its hard-earned money on that kind of research when Americans are willing to fund it? The Japanese are not fools. They know they don't develop that kind of talent in Japan. They would have to change their whole educational system and their national character to do the kind of research that comes so naturally to the West. It's not that the Japanese are afraid to spend money. They spend money on projects that have great potential for growth, on finding practical uses for new technology, or on projects that promise great future profits. The acquisition of a ten percent share of a tiny American company called Spacehab Corporation by six different Japanese companies serves as an excellent example of shrewd Japanese research investment. This little company plans to lease containers on spaceships so that scientists can conduct experiments under weightless conditions.

Those six Japanese companies are, incidentally, all members of the same Mitsubishi *keiretsu*. The Japanese will not even be ready to offer spacelab services for another six or seven years, but they are investing now to learn what must be done at each step along the way. Ten years from now Mitsubishi will either decide to buy Spacehab outright, or will have already learned everything that Spacehab has to teach and have reproduced the work somewhere in Japan. When these Japanese companies eventually sell their shares of Spacehab, they will also have made a profit on their "research" investment.

To get an idea of how adroitly the Japanese have learned to dance around politically sensitive trade issues while still keeping their eyes on their long-range goals, consider the U.S.-Japan satellite accord. The United States had been complaining that the Japanese government was not only refusing to buy American communications satellites, but was subsidizing research and development of Japanese satellites that ultimately would be used for commercial purposes. This is an unfair trade practice. Private American companies couldn't possibly compete with the entire Japanese government. So the U.S. government threatened them with a "Section 301" trade sanction, which was authorized by the Trade Act and approved by Congress in 1989.

In April 1990, the Japanese government backed down and announced that the Post and Telecommunications Ministry from then on would open the government satellite business to competitive bidding. The Japanese government would print its needs in official publications and let companies from all over the world bid. The United States Trade Representative's office was satisfied and declared that Japan was still a most favored nation and no "301" sanctions should be imposed.

The very next month, May of 1990, it was announced that a 13-company Japanese consortium led by Mitsubishi Heavy Industries, along with as many as 77 other companies, would develop a satellite-launching business.

Mitsubishi will produce the huge, liquid-fueled rocket called the H-II, a satellite launcher, that will rival the technology of Europe's Ariane services, the NASA program, as well as the programs offered by China and Russia. The first H-II is not scheduled for test launching until 1993, and it is feared by many that unless the Japanese govern-ment steps in to subsidize this effort, the Mitsubishi consortium services will not be competitively priced. But, Masato Yamano, president of Japan's National Space Development Agency (Nasda) says, "It is certainly not too early to think about providing our rockets to international markets."[20]

Yamano, in a press interview, stated that to build and launch an H-II rocket would probably cost more than 100 million dollars, a far higher expenditure than was spent by its competitors. It will lift a two-ton satellite into a high stationary orbit, which makes it a mid-range delivery vehicle, and leaves it out of the heavy-lift business. Thus, it seems that unless this consortium plans to operate with significant losses, they will need government subsidies to make the program work.

What happened to the promises of April? Granted, in April Japan was talking about satellites, while in May it was rockets to launch the satellites. Apples and oranges? Perhaps. However, the real issue is government subsidies to private business, not satellites and rockets. The point is that it's time for the United States to learn that it is struggling for its economic life. The days when a massive military landing force could be summoned up to confront lunatics like Saddam Hussein in Iraq are fast coming to an end. Americans can't afford it anymore. The United States no longer has an industrial base to support this kind of spending. President George Bush has made America's last hurrah with the Middle East task force, Operation Desert Storm, and he had to have outside contributions to make it work.

CHAPTER TWELVE

SPIES: The United States Trade Representative's Office

The Office of the United States Trade Representative was originally created as the Office of the Special Representative for Trade Negotiations by Executive Order on January 15, 1963. As part of the Trade Act of 1974, Congress established this department as an agency of the Executive Office of the President and charged it with administering the nation's trade agreements program. Some years later, the U.S.T.R. was also given responsibility for setting and administering overall U.S. trade policy.

Thus the U.S.T.R. assumes tremendous control over the foreign trade relations of the United States. The U.S.T.R. administers all relations with the General Agreement on Tariffs and Trade (GATT) and the Organization for Economic Cooperation and Development. It supervises American participation in every United Nations Conference on Trade and Development, and it controls implementation of the Trade Act's Section 301 punitive actions, which are used against nations engaged in unfair trade practices.

In effect, what has been created is a powerful agency with almost "ultimate authority." Unfortunately, this kind of power is best invested in agencies that have a strategic mandate. If the United States had a branch of government that functioned as the overall strategic planner for the nation's international trade and industrial needs, such as Japan's MITI, the U.S.T.R. would be a department within that organization. It would never be allowed to make decisions on its own. Until that time, the U.S.T.R. should be incorporated into the Commerce Department as a stopgap measure until the United States can create such a strategic branch.

The U.S.T.R. is a tactical trade agency with strategic powers. It has far too much responsibility. Congress must curb its power. At a bare minimum, there needs to be a congressional oversight function established to review U.S.T.R. decisions.

The charge that the U.S.T.R. is operated by people with apparently conflicting interests is made more meaningful when the backgrounds and financial interests of the people who lead this organization are brought to light. Carla Hills, as of this writing, holds the title of U.S. Trade Representative, a cabinet level appointment. She reports directly to the President. The fact that Hills once represented Matsushita Electric Industrial Co. in an anti-dumping complaint would not in itself disqualify her from the job.

But Hills' husband, Roderick, practices law with the head of Nissan Motor Company's lobbying firm, William Eberle, and in fact, is his law partner. According to a Wall Street Journal article, in 1988, Roderick Hills "lobbied to quash legislation proposed by Senator Alan Dixon, the Democrat from Illinois, that would have placed sanctions on C. Itoh as the exporter-of-record for the illegal sale of Toshiba milling equipment to the Soviet Union."[1] He denies the charge of influence peddling and claims that he was only doing C. Itoh a favor for no remuneration.

William Eberle was named to the U.S.T.R.'s Advisory Committee on Trade Policy and Negotiations early in the Bush Administration. To my knowledge, this has never before been reported publicly, but it is confirmed by the U.S.T.R. It appears that a lobbyist for Japan was helping to establish United States trade policy.

The Hills' daughter, Laura, is a lawyer and a registered foreign agent who recently represented a Japanese typewriter manufacturer being investigated by the Commerce Department for dumping.

The Wall Street Journal, which first broke this story, also reported that, "The Washington representative of Japan's leading trade organization is such a close Hills family friend that he attended the weddings of their children."[2] This friendship with C. Itoh's Washington representative, Takeshi Kondo, could well be seen as an informal channel of communication to the Japanese business community: C. Itoh's former chairman, Ryuzo Sejima, is the deputy chairman of the Tokyo Chamber of Commerce and a frequent advisor to MITI.

Imagine what would happen if a vice president of The Coca-Cola Company was discovered married to a lawyer representing the Pepsi-Cola Company in a patent infringement suit against, say, her own company. Then it was revealed that her daughter was also a lawyer representing Pepsi-Cola in another law suit against The Coca-Cola Company. Everybody is entitled to hire a lawyer. But, then it comes out that the vice president of public relations at Pepsi is such a close family friend of the Coca-Cola vice president that he has attended the weddings of her children... Did he bring a gift? It may well be very innocent, but it calls into question the ability of the Coca-Cola vice president to make objective decisions.

Lower in the U.S.T.R. organization at the time of *The Wall Street Journal* article was Sidney Linn Williams, a deputy trade representative, who handled Japan issues. Before taking this job, he was a corporation lawyer in Tokyo where he represented six Japanese companies. Since leaving the job he has joined a Washington law and lobbying firm. Another deputy in the U.S.T.R. is Julius Katz, who currently holds the rank of ambassador. He previously headed a consulting company that represented Toyota Motor Corporation and the Hitachi Research Institute.

Ishihara talks about having dinner with his friend Glen Fukushima, whom he identifies as the then-Deputy Assistant U.S. Trade Representative for Japan and China. In other words, Fukushima was the American most directly involved with the day-to-day-trade negotiations in this area. Ishihara tells us that Fukushima is one of America's most capable Asia specialists. "His wife is an intellectual Keio University graduate who prefers to live in Japan, forcing Glen to commute to Japan two or three times a month."[3] If this was truly the case, we need to ask who paid for all this commuting, and how can such a man know where his loyalties lie? On leaving the U.S.T.R. office, Fukushima joined A.T.& T. in Tokyo.

In describing a dinner conversation, Ishihara documents a very cozy relationship. "I...asked him what America's next Japan-bashing scenario would entail. He replied that the U.S. would take up the distribution issue...," meaning Japan's policy of blocking or limiting foreign merchandise.[4] But the real issue at this point is why Fukushima continued to dine and converse with a foreign government representative who was attacking the United States. "Japan-bashing," indeed! If Fukushima said anything to defend his own country, Ishihara did not report it. Thus, if Ishihara's account can be believed, it seems that Fukushima ought to learn some lessons in discretion and, perhaps, in loyalty to the nation he serves.

Ishihara tells us that Fukushima thought very highly of Makoto Kuroda, then vice-minister of international affairs, Ministry of International Trade and Industry. Fukushima was quoted as calling Kuroda one of Japan's best negotiators. The Japanese press itself used to criticize Kuroda's tough positions on the United States. They said that his attitudes aggravated trade relations, and the Americans thought he was too stubborn to deal with. But Kuroda knows how to say no, and this is seen as a virtue among the conservative factions in Japan, regardless of what the more liberal press thinks. Though why Fukushima should see it that way is anybody's guess. At minimum, this brothers-under-the-skin fraternization with our most aggressive trade partner is sending a wrong message to Japan. At worst, it smells of collusion.

It doesn't give U.S. corporations confidence in their own government to learn that tax-paid representatives are becoming so cozy with the enemy. John Taylor, Zenith Electronics Corporation's director of public relations, says that Japanese companies are still dumping televisions and VCRs in the United States and that there has been no help forthcoming from either the U.S.T.R or the Commerce Department.[5] America and Japan are competitors, in case the U.S.T.R. has forgotten that fact. Information leaks from the U.S.T.R. office are routine, and these have gone a long way towards destroying its credibility.

During the FSX fights in Congress, the Mitsubishi Corporation's lobbyist knew the results of the interagency negotiations before any of the results were publicly disclosed. When Hills was nominated to head the U.S.T.R., the first report was published not in an American newspaper, but in *Nihon Keizai Shimbun*, Japan's business daily.

Alan Wolff, a former lawyer at the U.S.T.R., was reported as saying that he once got a call from a Japanese official about the results of a White House cabinet meeting before his boss, Robert Strauss, had even completed the one block walk from the White House to his own office.

Even worse is the revolving employment door between the U.S.T.R. and the countries, companies and lobbyists with whom it negotiates. Clyde Prestowitz, a former Commerce Department official in the Reagan Administration, says, "If you are a government trade negotiator, you know sooner or later you'll leave government. Clearly it's not advantageous to make enemies."[6]

In reference to Patrick Choate's book *Agents of Influence*, a *New York Times* editorial suggested that lobbying, or buying influence is no reason to single out the Japanese. They are just doing what many American companies do.

The Japanese, however, do not return the privilege. In Japan, American companies cannot behave as Japanese companies do here. The problem is one of reciprocity. "The Japanese political system is far less open than that of the United States, with intimate ties between government ministries, industry and politicians. Foreigners are largely excluded from this tight triangle. This asymmetry could put American businesses at a considerable disadvantage."

"The remedy," according to *The New York Times*, "is not to put specific restrictions on Japan's lobbying in the United States, although tighter rules for all lobbyists, domestic and foreign, may well be justified. The better course is to persuade Tokyo to make its political system more open."[7] And here is the heart of the misunderstanding between the United States and Japan.

The New York Times has missed the point. The *Times* has often written with compelling logic of the need for equitable trade relations. It favors free trade, because that makes sense rationally. They are assuming that all men around the world share the same ideals of fairness and justice. In fact, what the *Times* is doing is asking the Japanese leopard to change its spots.

Japan will not change. Its political system will not become more open to satisfy the United States. Japan cannot change, because then it would become something other than Japanese. Patrick Choate is not the only person to recognize this fact. In Europe there are business and government leaders who are well aware of the economic danger from Japan and its political intractability.

Perhaps the shrewdest, most aware corporate executive today is Alain Gomez, chairman of the board of Thomson Group, France's largest electronics company. Gomez was quoted in *The New York Times* as saying, "The Japanese are waging a type of industrial war..." He concludes by saying, "The Japanese strategy of conquest is made easier by the gullibility, naiveté and weakness of the West."[8]

Yet France, unlike the U.S., has decided to fight back, to protect its markets and its production jobs. The Japanese don't like it. "The French are the flagship of European protectionism," says Takao Negishi, European director of the Electronics Industry Association of Japan, in the same article. "They're not playing the game according to the rules." Of course, Negishi never talks about the protected home markets in Japan.

In the United States, where the textile industry has been decimated by Japanese predatory pricing, there seemed, briefly in the fall of 1990, to be some hope for a tiny measure of relief. The U.S. Congress tried to pass a bill that would freeze leather shoe imports at 1989 levels and limit the growth of textile and clothing imports to one percent a year over the 1989 levels. But the bill was vetoed by President Bush, and enough support could not be generated in the Congress to override the veto.

In September 1990, four thousand union members showed up at a rally in Washington, D.C. to support the Textile Bill. They protested that the jobs of American low-paid textile and apparel workers were threatened by the proliferation of cheap Asian imports. In fact, over 500,000 American workers have lost their jobs in the textile industry in the past decade alone. The Fiber and Fabric Apparel Coalition for Trade, a group that represents textile companies and unions both, reports that "the industry has lost 60 percent of its market to foreign competition since 1980."[9]

Opponents of this textile bill said that Americans already pay about 250 dollars a year extra for their apparel because of protectionist legislation. If the bill were to pass, they argued that Americans would have had to pay 1,000 dollars more per year for clothing than without this protectionism.

These arguments about the inflationary effect on the cost of merchandise are completely specious. They do not address the fact that American men and women are being thrown out of work all over the country, that the United States is losing its manufacturing base in industry after industry. American workers would be happy to pay the extra 1,000 dollars if in turn they could land jobs that would also allow them to buy groceries.

While it was easy to be sympathetic to the purpose of the Textile Bill, namely, to protect American jobs, quotas are not the answer. They are too easily circumvented. Much higher tariffs will solve the problem of job-destroying imports. High tariffs allow essential products to enter the country while keeping out the unnecessary ones.

The number of long-term, permanently unemployed people in the United States is not tracked by the Labor Department anymore. Nor is it known with any certainty how many millions of underemployed people live in our nation's ghettos, rusting industrial areas and dying textile towns. The Census Department seems to have deliberately undercounted the poorest sections of this country. America has forgotten its own people by the millions, and doesn't want to be reminded about them.

The United States is spending billions of dollars on a futile drug war based on interdiction, that is, stopping the flow of goods before they hit the streets. Yet, as a nation, the U.S. seems perfectly willing to condemn more and more millions of displaced workers to the unemployment rolls, or to a future as hamburger flippers in fast food joints. From meaningful work, on which a person could see the value he added to a product, and see his skill usefully employed, millions of people are now mired in jobs of mindless routines or permanent idleness. Over nine million people are out of work in America. Is it any wonder that people lose their sense of self-esteem and slip into the numbing escape of drugs? Who could face such a future? Where is the hope for better times?

Representative Thomas Foglietta (D-Pennsylvania) argued for passage of the Textile Bill by reminding his fellow members of Congress that "80 percent of the shoes sold in America are foreign made. Almost 70 percent of the clothing bought by Americans is imported."[10]

Into this scenario steps the U.S. Trade Representative Carla Hills. The trouble in the textile industry is all the fault of junk-bond debt, she reports. "The industry has cried wolf for over 30 years. The reality is that they have continued to enjoy modest but steady growth throughout the years," her office reported to Congress.[11] Hills' office has turned a deaf ear to American workers. It seems she doesn't care how many millions of Americans in the textile and shoe industries are laid off and can't find work. This is an awfully heartless disregard for the people who pay Hills' wages. If American workers can't depend on their own government to look after their interests, to whom can they turn?

A basic principle that all nations should observe is begging to be expressed here. Namely, each country has to look after its own people, because one nation can't depend on another. And certainly no nation can depend on Japan. That's why we have nations and governments and not anarchy.

To be fair to Hills, she has never claimed to be an expert on trade matters. Prior to this job she was Secretary of Housing and Urban Development in the Ford Administration. She was also a lawyer in private practice specializing in antitrust law, and served on the boards of several large corporations. At best, Hills appears naive about the needs of American commerce and industry. At worst, she is another Washington political career opportunist.

Whatever Carla Hills is, her agency has been misguided in establishing its five principles:

1. A tariff-free world.
2. Reform agricultural trade.
3. Agree on rules of trade in services, investment and intellectual property.
4. Curb trade-distorting subsidies.
5. Integrate developing world into the trading system.

As fine sounding as the U.S.T.R.'s five principles are, they are utopian in a world where the principles of the Turkish bazaar reign supreme. When the goals are not idealistic, they are nebulous and unspecific. The poor nations of the world need tariff protection, and will not surrender it. Developing countries need subsidies to foster and protect nascent industries or fragile agricultural economies. It may be their only means of protecting their supply of scarce, hard currencies. Even industrial countries such as Japan need subsidies for their rice farmers to insure survival in the event of some future war. The Japanese might starve if all their rice came from overseas and the seas were cut off. In addition, industrial countries need tariffs to protect jobs for their own people and help their industries to grow and shield their own markets from too much foreign competition.

Americans ought to be asking what right any politician has to force workers to compete with Chinese or Malaysian workers who are thrilled to earn 50 cents an hour. What democratic ideal says America owes the world a living? Americans got lucky and occupy a mineral-rich and fertile land. The country can allow its people to live comfortably if they don't squander their heritage. But there is no moral imperative that says Americans have to let Japanese pick-up trucks into the United States, and then call them automobiles so that they can enjoy a lower tariff. Moreover, there is no reason to then reclassify the "automobiles" as trucks so that they can escape the EPA gasoline mileage requirements.[12] Yet, this is what the U.S. does for the Japanese in the spirit of free trade.

When Mitsubishi built its automobile plant in Illinois, they had enough political influence to get their plant declared a foreign trade zone, so that they could receive Japanese parts at prices below the American competition. That designation, not available to U.S. automobile manufacturers, entitled Mitsubishi to a reduction in its federal import duties.

What has happened in the United States in the past 10 to 15 years is a gradual, but consistent, erosion of the legal and competitive positions of domestic manufacturing companies in relation to those Japanese corporations that have invaded the United States. Neither the British, nor the Dutch, nor any other country has been as successful as the Japanese in molding U.S. laws and regulations to its advantage. But then again, our European allies do not control government agencies. They have never attempted to spend the vast amounts of money on buying influence that the Japanese do.

What is desperately needed in the United States is a 20-year plan for economic revitalization. The United States needs its own Marshall Plan: Some kind of strategic planning department of government that is empowered to set priorities for research and development. It should have the authority to guide trade policy, national investment strategy and to have a serious voice in national taxation policy. Actually, this department might work best as a joint branch of both houses of Congress, with key staff members being elected to their posts for two-year terms from the ranks of Congress itself. Staff appointments should not be based on the seniority system, but rather on fields of expertise. The idea is to make this agency responsible to the people on a regular basis. The President might also be allowed staff representation to better assure that all perspectives receive due consideration. The detailed arguments over national direction would take place within this agency, and its decisions would be subject to a vote by the entire Congress and to a veto by the President. Long-term economic strategy and policy for the country then would be set by elected representatives of the people, while the administrative function would be left to the Executive Branch.

Why should the American government decide to support research or product development in consumer electronics and not in improved dairy production? Why should it recommend that vast amounts of money be spent on vocational schools and in support of establishing apprenticeship programs, and not a comparable sum on music training? These are the types of questions that need to be discussed in such a government agency.

If there is a certain minimum level of tool making capability, or semiconductor capacity, necessary for national security, who decides that today? Is anybody even looking at the problem on a regular basis? What percent of American steel, and of which types, should be domestically produced? Shouldn't corporate profits, reinvestment plans and executive wages be regulated, especially in tariff protected industries? Can America afford to give away the trade secrets of its aviation industry simply to secure an order for a few airplanes?

There are answers to all of these questions. The problem is that nobody in the U.S. Congress, or in the White House, is asking the questions or forming any organizations or committees to address them.

CHAPTER THIRTEEN

SYMBIOSIS LOST:
The Growth of Parasitism

When any two nations become as economically involved with each other as are the United States and Japan, there is no way to avoid trade friction. Like it or not, the two economies have become inextricably intertwined. A relationship once built on complementary trade has become ferociously competitive so that the countries' national interests often collide. The Japanese have become the basic manufacturing source for the United States, while the United States provides Japan with raw materials, food and basic research. This is a complete reversal of the pre-War trade patterns. Thus the symbiosis has been lost. In its place has grown a parasitical relationship. The Japanese have become parasites feasting on the sap of American ingenuity and generosity under the protection of our strong military branches.

This is not a criticism of the Japanese; they have done nothing wrong. They were invited to the picnic by the Americans and simply stayed to enjoy the meal. Perhaps Japanese table manners leave a little to be desired, but then again, the United States has long been accustomed to making allowances, even for guests who stuff themselves. The United States' error was to extend the invitation in the first place.

In an article entitled "Japan Isn't Playing by Different Rules," Professor Michael E. Porter of the Harvard Business School attributes this deterioration in our trade relationship to America's move away from faith in competition.[1] He's right, but

Japan, in fact, does play by different rules. Japanese home markets are closed to outsiders by various regulations and distribution associations; whole industries are subsidized; dumping is a way of life in their export world and tariff protection is standard procedure.

Each country has also had different strategies for growth. The United States was more preoccupied with world security needs and cold war politics and the consequent need to build its military-industrial complex. Because of this fact, the nations devastated by World War II were able to concentrate their efforts on rebuilding their civil economic infrastructures and consumer industries. To aid in their recoveries, the United States opened its markets to them, and provided the Marshall Plan and other investment programs.

For years, the majority of America's federally supported research and development funds were spent on military or space projects. America was in a race for survival, or so it was believed, with the Communist menace. The Western world looked to the United States for protection. Year after year, graduating classes of engineers and scientists were lured to the defense industry to work on avionics, missile guidance systems, reentry thermodynamics and high density particle beams.

Some marvelous benefits of this work filtered down to the commercial world and, ultimately, to the consumer. The trouble is that this work was all done for exclusive government contracts. There was no competition to develop, say, a safer nuclear submarine engine. A contract was given, and the Navy supervised the development. It was an in-house operation. The result is that General Dynamics' Electric Boat Division doesn't know how to bid on a non-government ship building job today. They never learned how to compete. This is true in most heavy industries, and it explains why America has been losing its market share.

The trouble with the United States' research and development system is that it breeds a collegiality, a clubbiness among the insiders. When there is no competition, there is no fear of losing the order. Consequently, cost overruns, quality problems and production delays have become standard features of the military-industrial complex. Worse, the standards and attitudes set by leading companies with all the research money have been picked up by the consumer products companies. "Let the buyer beware, I've got a quarterly report due next week," is the tune.

What has happened is that the ability of the United States to compete in world trade has eroded, especially in heavy industries and other manufacturing operations where complicated tooling is required. "Eighty-five percent of all American exports are still accounted for by only 15 percent of American companies. Half the firms that do export are active in only one market."[2] Corporate managers and executives have become indolent and rich, and are reluctant to take any product development or marketing risks that might jeopardize their bonuses. Today's imaginative executive only applies new coats of paint to old products. Ordinary executives don't even do this. Management has become a skill of holding on to the status quo. For them, innovation is risky business and something to be avoided lest the quarterly reports be damaged.

Is it any wonder that the American organism has been infested with parasites? Thirty years ago, a Cadillac was the ideal luxury car for Americans. Today, it's a Mercedes or the infuriatingly misspelled Infiniti. There was a time when Kodak film didn't have any competition. Today it has Fuji and a raft of foreign-made private labels. MCA, Columbia Pictures, and

Rockefeller Center are not even American companies anymore, along with many others that have fallen.

This situation will not change by itself. American corporate executives are not going to give up their bonuses. If any changes are to be made, they will have to be forced on industry by the U.S. Congress. In the meantime, Japan will continue to take advantage of America's military-inspired technology and its university-based research, and produce highly competitive consumer products that will drive even more U.S. corporations into bankruptcy and foreign ownership.

The Bush Administration should also recognize that any more cowardly maneuvers to reduce the value of the dollar, or to convince foreign governments to increase their arms purchases, are certain to be self-defeating. We have come too far along that path already. Simply decreasing the prices of American products is not a long-term solution to the problem. New products are needed. The only way to stop the flight of manufacturing jobs out of the country is to develop exclusive new industries and improved new products, and to then protect them from foreign competition. America doesn't need any more foreign-owned plants. They are only a symptom of the failed economic policies of the past. The military-industrial sector must now take the back seat and submit to a rebirth of civil development.

The subject of an American strategic planning organization for trade and industrial matters was discussed in the last chapter. It is daily becoming more evident, in fact, that the entire function of government in the United States needs to be reviewed. The Executive Branch, led by only one elected official, has by force of personality, rather than by any constitutional mandate, taken responsibility for the nation's strategic planning. What this amounts to is that thousands of appointed civil servants are guiding America with no written agenda. They are, instead, making up their own plans as they go along. Thus, oddly enough, administrators have had to assume responsibility for policy and planning, and that's a serious mistake. The people need to decide where the United States is going.

Congress has seen its responsibility in very narrow terms until now. As guardians of the treasury, the Congress appropriates funds. But this power has largely been used to withhold funds from unworthy projects or to support programs on which a consensus has been reached. Nowhere are national programs made to fit into an overall strategic scheme for the nation's future.

What kind of a country does America hope to be in 20 years? How should Americans earn their livings in the year 2012? How important will a huge military establishment be in the future, and what should the United States role be in terms of the world's peacekeeper? Is a true national health care program something that America wants? If so, how will it be financed? How does America plan to improve its schools? These and many other questions need to be asked and answered. National budgets need to be approved on a five-year basis with annual discussion of the fifth year's budget, not the next year's.

Life in the nuclear age has become far too complex to allow the future of the United States to be determined by appointed bureaucrats however well-meaning they are, or by ad hoc committees. The Congressional committee system is currently so bogged down with appropriations bills that annual budget approvals have become excrutiating and frustrating procedures. Intelligent men and women who have gone to Washington with all good hopes of serving their country have found themselves instead wrangling over picayune issues affecting local military bases and tobacco subsidies. The amount of time Congresspeople devote to important issue of national destiny consists of pathetic minutes instead of the great national debates that are required.

Into this morass have stepped the opportunistic Japanese. They have a plan, and part of this plan is not to allow lowly delegates at international conferences to negotiate final dispositions to trade problems. Japanese politics are heavily influenced by local special-interest groups. These groups have become expert at working with each other to block adverse legislation and to promote policies favorable to domestic growth. The result is that Japanese politicians, including the prime minister, are often made to look like liars in the world of diplomacy. A government minister or negotiator in Japan must always reflect his nation's strategic goals; otherwise he or she runs the risk of looking foolish in the press.

It would be good for Western negotiators to remember this point. When returning from a round of talks and thinking that at last they have reached an accord with the Japanese, they should probably ask what their Japanese counterpart actually agreed to. The chances are that the Japanese negotiator avoided saying no. Instead, he probably smiled a lot and suggested that a satisfactory solution could be easily reached. It is important to leave such a conference with a concrete response, not just a smile, if one plans to take any action based on the conference's outcome.

Part of Japan's strategy is that national issues cannot be negotiated on a national level. The structure of its government doesn't allow for it. This policy insures that any changes that affect the nature or destiny of Japan will have to be debated at the levels at which people are affected. (Anybody who has ever worked with a Japanese company will understand this fact. In microcosm, a company reflects its larger government. A division president, for example, is often not the chief executive officer.

The real boss may not even have a title. He might be tucked away, out of view, in the accounting department.) In government, a prime minister such as Toshiki Kaifu, who had no bureaucratic or industrial power base of his own, is always a weak leader. Generally, the real power is not invested in any one person, even if he has a power base, but shared by people in a combination of departments, in MITI or, deceptively, out of the government entirely.

Japan must have a healthy host upon which to live. When one host begins to fail, it is essential to Japanese strategy that it begin to infiltrate another. The opening to Eastern Siberia that Japan has long sought, and the first step toward the building of its self-sufficiency in Asia, is, in the final analysis, more important than the return of four insignificant islands. Once Japan has a toe-hold in Siberia, and can start pumping in waves of people to staff its new operations, it can always retake those islands whenever it becomes convenient. There is no strategic imperative that mandates the return of those properties, at least, not in the same sense that strategy demands a Japanese presence in Siberia. Boris Yeltsin should remember this point.

Already, in anticipation of grand changes in world relationships, the Japanese are beginning to demand that U.S. debt be issued in Japanese yen rather than in inflation-prone dollars. They are tired of bailing out America and being repaid in ever more worthless greenbacks. Japan suspects that its post-War host is failing. The Japanese see a social and economic weakness in the United States that disturbs them. They don't wonder whether America can continue to lead the free world, but if it can continue to buy Japan's products.

Morita screams that it is time to tell the United States that it is on the verge of bankruptcy. Clearly, the relationship between Japan and the United States is in serious trouble.

Because of its cultural heritage, Japan has remained silent up until now. The Japanese have passed along only whispers of their concern. But it is time now to insist upon changes in America's economic policies, Morita warns. If change does not start happening soon in America, Japan will pay the heaviest price. He believes that Japan is too heavily invested in the United States and too reliant on American markets as an outlet for its manufactured goods and as a source for raw materials. Japan relies on trade to survive, and the outlook for future profitable relationships with the United States is growing dimmer. Without trade, the Japanese fear losing their identity as a people.

CHAPTER FOURTEEN

SUMMARY: Some Answers

The destiny of the United States need not be written in Japan. America can recover its position of economic primacy in the world. It can resurrect its manufacturing industries and provide worthwhile jobs for its people. The last chapter on the United States has not yet been written. There is a way out.

Morita and Ishihara unwittingly opened a Pandora's box with their book and allowed the ills of the commercial world to be examined in the light of day. Unfortunately for Japan, by exposing to the world many of the faults and weaknesses of the United States, their book forces Americans to review the history of trade relations between the two countries. It also challenges Americans to take a close look at the patterns of Japanese tariffs and exclusionary import restrictions, and at Japan's internal distribution systems that so effectively discriminate against foreign competitors. It prods Americans to examine the history of the Japanese dumping of products in American markets by means that would have landed an American executive in jail. It causes America to look at the system of government subsidies to private business that gives an unfair competitive advantage to Japanese companies. How can a single corporation, even a large one, hope to compete with the resources of the Japanese government?

In the course of this examination we have become more aware of Japan's disruption of the United States' government and social structure. The limits of Japanese influence in American politics have not yet been tested. We have found entire departments of American government to be in the hands of Japanese policymakers. We have seen, thanks to Patrick Choate and his book, *Agents of Influence*, the extent of Japanese success in buying influence.

The Japanese have not been quite as successful with these tactics in Europe as they have been in America. For some reason, European governments take a more proprietary interest in international trade than do the Americans. They seem to better understand that the economic health of a nation is tied to its trade decisions. Moreover, these countries take a more protective attitude toward their own industries, realizing that a healthy manufacturing sector is vital to providing work for their people.

Since the 1930s, the United States has been slavishly devoted to a policy of free trade. For a short period after World War II there was some benefit to be gained from this policy. It was important to help our allies and former enemies regain their economic feet by opening the great American market to them. But that need has long since passed. Today, America's free trade policy is seen by the rest of the world as an extraordinary opportunity. A comment that is often heard overseas is, "If the United States allows itself to be taken advantage of, what kind of fools would we be not to take the advantage?"

With a Pacific base, the Japanese have all the labor nearby that they could ever possibly use. Conceivably, Japan could manufacture everything needed by the world. All they need is time.

Japan is full of vinegar these days. The whole country is enjoying the fruits of its labor and of its brilliant planning. Even an economic slowdown in Japan amounts only to relatively slower growth, not the terrible factory closings and unemployment that results in the United States. It's only natural that Japan should flex its muscles a little bit and bay at the moon.

If the United States ever hopes to rejoin the race for world economic dominance, or even to secure a competitive position in that race, then it will have to reverse years of wasteful profligacy. It began years ago when Lyndon Johnson claimed that America could afford both guns and butter. It was his Administration that sent domestic social spending skyrocketing, and at the same time dumped America into a bottomless pit in Vietnam that eventually cost billions of dollars and took hundreds of thousands of lives, and sapped the moral strength of the whole nation. Government led by the Nixon Administration was no better. Under a flag-waving and insane hyper-patriotism it compounded the problem. Ignoring the needs of the nation's business, Americans spent years fighting each other in the streets over involvement in Indochina. Meanwhile, the Japanese gobbled up America's markets.

However, there is plenty of blame that can be passed around, and it's not just America's political leaders who should take the rap. The United States has become a greedy nation. There is a different attitude in the country today than there was thirty years ago. In the 1950s, basketball players could read and write, baseball players did not make five million dollars a year, and savings and loan associations were not allowed to invest in junk bonds. There was a progressive income tax that made it hard for one person to become so rich that Croesus would be envious.

As a people Americans today accept these changes, allowing individual athletes to be cheated of an education, allowing the schools to be corrupted just so a team can win a pennant. Few question the government that deregulates the trucking industry, and ends up with low-cost freight rates at the expense of truckers who cannot afford to replace worn-out brakes. Few question the deregulation of the airlines that end in a bankrupt industry that cheats on its aircraft safety inspections. Competition is believed to be a God-given mandate that applies equally in all situations. It doesn't. There is a time and a place for everything, including federal regulation of certain industries. And when major changes in existing institutions are being considered, there ought to be a two-year waiting period before new laws can change them. Time is needed to think through the consequences of actions.

Americans ignore, en masse, their duty as citizens and avoid the bother of voting. Less than 55 percent of the nation's registered voters participated in the 1988 Presidential election. This is one of the lowest voter turnouts in the industrialized world. It's not "moral malaise" as much as it is indifference. And that is the nub of America's immorality. A spiritual awakening is needed that will help the country to again find its sense of values. Learning to look outward at the world's needs, accepting responsibility for the condition of one's fellow citizens, and learning a little humility are important values for a great nation to espouse. A "thousand points of light" has turned out to be an empty commitment.

In March 1992, Nielsen Media Research reported that in America, people aged 18 and over watch an average of 4.5 hours of television daily. Neil Postman, a professor at New York University, wrote, "In [Aldous] Huxley's vision, no Big Brother is required to deprive people of their autonomy, maturity and history. As he saw it, people will come to love their oppression, to adore the technologies that undo their capacities to think."[1] Truth, and whatever else matters in life, is being drowned in a video sea of irrelevance and nonsense. Television is a black hole that is sucking up the nation's time and brains.

■ AS A NATION America has to start doing again what it does best. That is, for example, oil companies should explore for oil or spend their money researching better ways to extract the oil already owned. They should not be allowed to buy department stores. The whole field of mergers and acquisitions needs to be re-evaluated along with the concomitant junk bond financing. At one time, International Telephone and Telegraph owned the Burpee Seed Company and Wonder Bread (Continental Baking). Can this possibly make any sense? Simultaneously, the Japanese at Sony were spending their surplus capital learning how to make semiconductors. Today, ITT is out of the gardening business and still struggling. Sony is a giant.

■ SHORT-TERM capital gains ought to be taxed at one-and-a-half times ordinary income taxes to penalize gamblers and other stock market speculators. Long-term capital gains ought to be taxed on a reducing scale so that, after ten years, the tax would dwindle to four or five percent. The point here is that the United States can no longer afford to waste its national wealth on making a privileged class of speculators rich. The whole field of options trading, computerized program trading and "junk bond" financing has to be curbed. Far too much money is being directed into these essentially short-term, highly traded markets.

Commodities hedging has a long and honorable place in the market. That is not the problem. The problem occurs when banks and institutions controlling huge pension funds join in the short-term speculation. If S & Ls cannot make a profit on home mortgages, and if commercial banks suddenly need to invest in stocks to find enough income opportunities, then it is time to review the circumstances that led to this situation. The solution is not to degrade investment portfolios, but rather to correct the underlying economy that caused the problem. That's like blaming the chickens for getting eaten by the fox when it was the farmer who left the gate open. For this reason, the Treasury Department's current plan to reorganize the banking industry fails—it treats the portfolio and not the market.

■ THE UNITED STATES needs an investment strategy. It could begin by establishing a Department of Industry that would fight for the long-term needs of America's manufacturing sector. It should be modelled after Japan's Ministry of International Trade and Industry. It would protect developing American industries, and encourage the legislation of incentives for the promotion of long-term investment goals beneficial to the nation. And these needs can be broadly defined. It would incorporate the existing Departments of Commerce and Labor and the Office of the U.S. Trade Representative. It would operate as a separate entity from the Congressional strategic planning organization mentioned in Chapter Twelve. However, under no circumstances should the government get into the business of production planning or any other tactical activity. The government's role is to set broad national goals and then to create laws and incentives that encourage production.

■ AMERICA NEEDS to increase the rate of personal savings. At four percent savings annually, which is about its average performance over the past ten years, America is a piker. Most of the industrialized world saves far more. Without savings, there is no money for long-term investments. It may be time to reconsider the idea of implementing a value-added tax in order to curb consumer spending. Certainly, if the imposition of tariffs does not curb the flow of needless imports, the VAT route will have to be considered. A tax on consumer credit purchases might even be a better idea. These notions are anathema in most parts of the United States, but a Congress less concerned about getting reelected might be more willing to tackle the structural economic problems of the country rather than just fiddling with placebos.

■ CONSEQUENTLY, Americans should consider restricting the length of time that any one person can serve in an elected political office. Already, there are limits on the President to two terms. Now it is time to trim the power of Congress. Senators should be held to two terms or 12 years and representatives to five terms or ten years. These changes are not as draconian as they may seem. Two thirds of the membership of Congress changes every ten years anyway. It is the deeply entrenched one third of the membership that needs to be cleaned out. This one third benefits from a rigid seniority system that heightens their power while making it more difficult for new Congresspeople to effect change. If elected officials understood in advance that Americans do not want them going to Washington to carve out a career, then more people might run for office who are truly qualified and committed to redressing America's problems.

A few states had voter initiatives on the ballot in 1990 to limit Congressional terms, but the idea was so new that voters felt uncomfortable with the propositions. They were voted down. In time, as the idea gets discussed more widely, this proposal will have a much better chance of success.

■ AMERICANS NEED to reduce their dependence on high-volume imported products. A tax on gasoline at the pump might initally boost inflation, but it would go a long way towards reducing America's trade imbalance and national debt. It would also have a tremendous beneficial result which would more than offset the temporary inflationary pressure: If the funds were actually used to lower the nation's debt, real interest rates would begin to fall and the economy would be greatly stimulated. It would encourage conservation and the search for alternative energy sources. The five-cents tax added in 1990 was a good start, but it is a fifty-cents tax that is really needed over the next few years.

■ GEORGE BUSH's Presidency has demonstrated that the United States cannot afford to continue its reign as the world's policeman. The expense of the confrontation with Iraq has been enormous and far beyond the ability of U.S. citizens to pay. It will be years before the true cost has been calculated. Just think of the thousands of tanks and helicopters and fighter planes that have worn out so quickly and that the services will want to replace. Imagine the Pentagon budget requests that are yet to come and the domestic needs that will have to be overlooked.

In spite of the collapse of the Soviet Union, the U.S. defense budget has hovered around 300 billion dollars since 1989, after an enormous run-up in the Reagan years from a 1980 budget of about 140 billion dollars. The Bush defense budget takes no account of the reduced threat to U.S. national security. It continues the strategy of being ready to fight a two-ocean war, a major and a minor land conflict, and the maintenance of hundreds of thousands of American troops overseas.

The time has come to reconsider the need for American troops and bases in Europe, Japan, The Philippines and Korea. A naval base at Guam in the western Pacific Ocean, and a cooperative base with European allies at Diego Garcia in the Indian Ocean ought to be sufficient to take care of strategic defense needs. More than that presupposes an offensive striking power, and now that the Cold War is over, there is no reason to pour money into offensive first-strike capabilities. It is no longer America's business, if ever it was, to assure that Vietnam maintains a capitalistic economy and friendly government.

Regional conflicts will have to be settled regionally from now on. The United States can no longer afford the luxury of putting out the world's fires. If South Korea and North Korea can't maintain friendly relations, that is not an American problem. The fact is, there has never been a South Korean government that was worth the cost of one American life. America has given up lives and a fortune to support one ruthless Korean regime after another, only to wind up with an ally that is angry because America attempts to keep its trade deficit with them from growing any larger.

■ CORPORATIONS in America today, and their shareholders, are hostages to overpaid, ineffective managers. Regardless of the explanations, it's obscene to read that Steven Ross, Chairman and co-C.E.O. of Time Warner, was paid almost 100 million dollars in 1991. Laws should be enacted to make recall of either management or directors easier. The corporate president who hasn't set his company on a long-term research and development program to support future growth ought to be demoted to the shops again. There should be laws forbidding corporations to develop "poison pills" and "golden parachutes." These are devices that serve only to protect entrenched, greedy managers from financial loss. These tricks seldom include protection for the workers in plants that might close.

■ NEW LABOR LAWS should be implemented that make it harder to terminate a worker. Medical benefits for long service employees must be protected. Top management is well provided for, but the workers, and many middle managers, are burdened by "employment-at-will" laws that leave them without recourse to unfair layoffs and dismissals. Severance pay must become a matter of law. Active workers deserve job security. How can a worker plan to participate in American life if the possibility of being fired—for no reason and almost no warning—always exists? Retirement benefits, once deposited to the pension fund, ought to be inviolable. Today, they are robbed in good times and never replaced in bad times. These benefits are treated as general corporate assets free for the spending by the simple device of changing an actuarial table. Retirees ought to have the security and benefit of improved curcumstances when their companies prosper.

A livable minimum wage is critical to the long-term stability of America's work force. It should be more advantageous to work than to receive unemployment compensation or welfare. The minimum wage in 1992 does not accomplish that goal.

The bill passed in 1990 requiring 60 days' notice of plant closings was a pittance thrown to labor in lieu of doing something of real value. A plant closing needs to be treated as a major national catastrophe that draws special attention from the Administration.

■ PRODUCT QUALITY and improved customer service must become higher priorities for American business. Americans used to laugh at the poor quality of Japanese products. Today, the most reliable products in the world come from Japan. It's a lesson Americans should never forget. Quality sells. If the truth were told, Ralph Nader is probably the best friend American business ever had. All he ever asked for was a quality product, and if it broke soon after being purchased, that it be fixed or replaced. What's so anti-business about that?

■ FINANCING and tax incentives are needed to support a massive research and development and production program in advanced semiconductor technology. America must regain this lead. The effort should also include superconductors and the whole field of robotics. Sematech, the current joint venture between government and business, should be encouraged. Applications research is also of primary importance. And once America makes scientific breakthroughs in the laboratories, it must quickly figure out ways to market these developments. University research is important, but it works best when it is unregulated and unfettered. Academics do wonderfully well at basic research, but seem to have no interest in applications reseach. Business must improve its communications with academia so that when new technology emerges, American engineers are the first to begin planning practical uses. Also, Americans are going to have to reconcile the gift of university research efforts to national competitors with its need to protect jobs and markets at home. A way must be found to protect American inventions and innovations.

■ THE DOCTRINE of free trade is a notion that ought to be buried. What is needed now, and has long been needed, are people in government who understand that only a reciprocal trade policy will keep America's economy afloat. America needs trading partners who will buy from it, within reasonable limits, about the same dollar amounts as it buys from them. It makes no sense to support a five billion dollar trade deficit with a country like the People's Republic of China. It's criminal to support a mad, tyranical government like that at the expense of U.S. jobs. Where's the benefit? Why encourage dictators who slaughter innocent people in the streets?

How can the United States justify a 40 to 50 billion dollar annual trade deficit with Japan? It can't. It's that simple. There is no reasonable explanation for this sad state of affairs. Japan, Korea, Taiwan, India, China, Brazil and a few others have simply taken advantage of America's trade policies. It has to stop. The quickest, most effective way to reduce these ridiculous trade deficits is to impose increased tariffs on all manufactured goods imported from those countries where the American trade deficit exceeds ten percent. If, for example, new import tariffs of 50 percent of the invoice value are imposed on all Japanese manufactured goods, the laws of economics would begin to cure America's trade problems. Critical goods would continue to flow while unnecessary merchandise would begin to dry up or be available only to the wealthy.

■ THE CITIZENS of the United States must learn again how to be effective salespeople. It's long past time that Americans go on the road for a living. It's time to reprice our products based on the economies of scale that will be had with improved sales and to take advantage of the reduced value of the dollar. The idea that 100 percent of tooling costs must be recouped in the first year is an anti-trade policy. There ought to be tax credits for profits generated by exports, and American embassies abroad ought to be reporting on trade opportunities and making those sometimes critical business introductions. Americans need to look at the overseas markets and begin to practice the salesperson's Golden Rule: America's markets will open if foreign markets are open to America.

Reciprocal trade is the direction the U.S. needs to follow, not free trade. Americans must tell the Japanese that the United States will begin to close its borders unless the Japanese open up trade opportunities. But Americans cannot rely solely on government action. That is always far too slow for business. American corporations need to get their sales efforts going now. This also applies to America's banking community. Over 20 percent of the U.S. commercial loan market has been snatched up in the past five years by Japanese and other foreign banks. If market share strategy works for the Japanese, it will work for the United States.

At this point, there is little choice but to start fighting back. It's either that or watch America's way of life begin to degenerate into despair and depression. The United States of America was made for better things.

Finally, we should express our gratitude to Akio Morita and Shintaro Ishihara. Whether purposely or not, they have done more to outline America's political and economic problems than anybody else in recent memory. They have also gone a long way towards showing Americans how to cure America's economic ills.

NOTES

CHAPTER ONE

1. "American-Japanese Trade: Its Structure and Significance," William W. Lockwood, *The Annals of the American Academy*, May 1941.

2. *Direction of Trade Statistics Yearbook*, 1991, International Monetary Fund.

3. Shintaro Ishihara, *The Japan That Can Say No*, 1991, p. 40.

4. The unauthorized version of *The Japan That Can Say No*, which circulated at Harvard University, and which was labeled "Kobunsha Kappa-Holmes", page 35, uses the word spy. In the official translation, on page 36, the comment reads, "After my sharp disagreement with Verity, Yeutter's man (U.S.T.R.) winked at me as if to say, 'Hang in there.' I smiled, thinking to myself, 'The United States is not so united after all.'"

5. Ishihara, on page 66 of the unauthorized translation of his book says, "The normalization of relations with China, by-passing Japan, set a precedent and provided a basis for other such threats to Japan by the U.S."

In the official version of *The Japan That Can Say No*, p. 52, the passage reads, "Now the Americans are threatening to pull a similar end run with the Soviet Union (Or the new commonwealth). They say, in effect, "We can establish a close relationship with Moscow before you even realize what is going on, as we did with Beijing, and then we won't need Japan anymore.'"

6. A 41 billion dollar trade deficit in 1990, due to the recession in the United States and some increased commodities imports by Japan. U.S. Department of Commerce, 1991.

7. *Direction of Trade Statistics Yearbook*, 1991, International Monetary Fund.

8. Edwin O. Reischauer, *The Japanese*, Belknap Press, 1977, p. 160.

9. Shintaro Ishihara, *The Japan That Can Say No*, 1991, p.54.

10. See note 5.

11. Akio Morita, *The Japan That Can Say No*, 1990, Unauthorized translation.

12. *Business Asia*, June 22, 1987, p.193.

CHAPTER TWO

1. Bank of Japan, reported in *The New York Times*, 12/29/91, D1.

2. Ministry of International Trade and Industry, Japan, Industrial Mining Index, reported in *The New York Times*, June 28, 1990, p. D2.

3. *The Wall Street Journal*, "Slower Growth For Japan", 6/12/91, International News Summary page.

4. Shintaro Ishihara, *The Japan That Can Say No*, p. 20, authorized translation.

5. Shintaro Ishihara, *The Japan That Can Say No*, 1990, Unauthorized translation. The official translation closely matches the quote in this case: "Semiconductors are the key to leadership in electronics, and competitive, high-volume production is the key to leadership in semiconductors." See page 21.

6. Shintaro Ishihara, *The Japan That Can Say No*, 1991, p.24.

CHAPTER THREE

1. U.S. Bureau of Labor Statistics

2. *The New York Times*, November 4, 1990, Op-Ed page.

3. *The New York Times*, September 2, 1990, Op-Ed page.

4. Ibid.

5. Compiled by the American Iron and Steel Institute, 1990, using Department of Commerce reports.

6. U.S. Bureau of Labor Statistics, May 1991.

7. *The New York Times*, December 25, 1991, p. 1.

8. *The New York Times*, November 11, 1990, p. 24.

9. General Electric Company, Notice of 1990 Annual Meeting and Proxy Statement.

10. A portion of this amount is bonus earned in 1989, but not payable until 1990.

11. Bonuses earned from 1987 through 1989 and payable in 1989.

12. Potential stock gain based on shares owned or controlled or available through stock option plans.

13. *The New York Times*, February 2, 1992, p. F1.

14. *The New York Times*, July 15, 1990, p. F 11, "Too Many Bosses, Too Few Workers," by Richard Rosecrance

15. Ibid.

16. Ibid.

17. Akio Morita, *The Japan That Can Say No*, Chapter Three, Unauthorized translation.

18. *The New York Times*, November 4, 1990, p. F 1, "American brokers arrived...," by James Sterngold.

19. *The Wall Street Journal*, March 26, 1991, p. B 8, Special Advertising Section, Global Financial Outlook, A Report from Tokyo.

20. *The Philadelphia Inquirer*, November 25, 1991, p. 1, "Hawaii sees Japanese investment...," by John Woestendick.

21. Bank of Japan, 1992.

CHAPTER FOUR

1. *Time*, October 8, 1990, "There Goes the Neighborhood," p.61.

2. *The Wall Street Journal*, July 23, 1990, p. A12, "Japanese Visas Prove Elusive..."

3. Shintaro Ishihara, *The Japan That Can Say No*, p. 26. Official translation, 1991.

4. Shintaro Ishihara, *The Japan That Can Say No*, p. 32, Official translation, 1991.

5. Shintaro Ishihara and Akio Morita, *The Japan That Can Say No*, 1990, Unauthorized translation. In the official version, these few lines are attenuated to read, "Japanese should realize that we have finally reached the position, thanks to our technology, where we can and must make an enormous contribution to U.S. security."

CHAPTER FIVE

1. *The New York Times*, May 13, 1990, Sect. 3, p. F13.

2. *The Economist*, July 7, 1990, "Moonlight and Bonsais," p. 44

3. *The Japanese Power Game*, William J. Holstein, p. 206.

4. *The New York Times*, "Talking Deals" by Paul Judge, October 11, 1990, p. D2.

5. *In These Times*, January 22-28, 1992, p. 3. by David Moberg.

6. *The Wall Street Journal*, "Strained Alliance," June 19, 1990, p. A1.

7. *The Wall Street Journal*, "Strained Alliance," June 13, 1990, p. A1.

8. Ibid.

9. Ibid.

CHAPTER SIX

1. Bank of Japan, 1992.

2. *The Wall Street Journal*, "U.S. Studies Sale of Hercules Unit to Japanese," June 15, 1990, p. A5.

3. *The Courier Times*, "Japan's Powerful Business Alliances Blasted," from the Associated Press, June 25, 1990, p. 7C.

4. Ibid.

CHAPTER SEVEN

1. National Science Foundation

2. *The New York Times* on March 1, 1992, page E7, in an article titled "Another Losing Battle With Japan?", argues that if calculated at market exchange rates for the yen, the Japanese spent $61.83 billion for research in 1989 or roughly 87 percent of what American business spent. The Japanese calculate that they spent $71.10 billion on research which is about equal with U.S. spending.

3. *The Wall Street Journal*, June 25, 1990, "Strained Alliances," p. A1.

4. *National Review*, November 4, 1991, "Punitive Damages," p. 16.

5. Akio Morita, *The Japan That Can Say No*, Chapter Five, 1990, Unauthorized translation.

6. Ibid.

7. *The New York Times*, July 8, 1990, p. E3.

8. *Timber from the South Seas*, J.M. Nectoux & R. Kuroda, 1989, World Wildlife Fund International, 1989, Switzerland.

9. *The New York Times*, July 8, 1990, p. E3.

10. The aerospace industry is the notable exception. They lead the country in exporting manufactured airplanes.

CHAPTER EIGHT

1. *The New York Times*, June 17, 1990, "Does Visionary Business Call for a Corporate Sage?," p. H 16.

2. *The Japanese Power Game*, William J. Holstein, p. 145.

3. Ibid.

4. *Fortune Magazine*, May 21, 1990, "Manufacturing the Right Way," p. 54.

5. Ibid.

6. Shintaro Ishihara, *The Japan That Can Say No*, 1990, Unauthorized translation.

7. Shintaro Ishihara, *The Japan That Can Say No*, 1991, p. 36.

CHAPTER NINE

1. Akio Morita, *The Japan That Can Say No*, 1990, Unauthorized translation.

CHAPTER TEN

1. Baron Reijiro Wakatsuki, *Foreign Affairs*, July 1935, p. 60.

2. Tyler Dennet, *Annals of the American Academy*, May 1941, "Japan's 'Monroe Doctrine' Appraised," p. 61.

3. Liberia still has the greatest number of ships, and the greatest tonnage, but these are really ships from many nations all trying to skirt liability and labor laws or to hide ownership. *Jane's Fighting Ships*, 1990-91.

4. I would use nonsexist language here and say salespeople, but in this capacity the Japanese don't use women in enough numbers to warrant a change in the language.

5. Office of Management and Budget, 1992.

6. *The New York Times*, March 1, 1992, "Another Losing Battle With Japan?," p. E7.

7. *The Wall Street Journal*, June 15, 1990, "Strained Alliance...," p. A1.

8. Ibid.

9. Akio Morita, *The Japan That Can Say No*, 1990, Unauthorized translation.

10. Ibid.

CHAPTER ELEVEN

1. *Jane's Fighting Ships*, Ninety-second edition, 1989-1990, p. 93. Since the dissolution of the Soviet Union, Japan may well have the world's second largest military budget.

2. This estimate by the Russian Embassy in Washington is probably high. The former Soviet Union was already disintegrating, and military spending was severely curtailed. The U.S. budget figure does not include the costs of Desert Shield and Desert Storm.

3. *The New York Times*, "For Japan's Military, Some Second Thoughts...," July 29, 1990, p. 3.

4. Shintaro Ishihara, *The Japan That Can Say No*, 1991, p. 53.

5. Shintaro Ishihara, *The Japan That Can Say No*, 1990, Unauthorized translation. In the official version of his book, on page 54,

the quote reads, "A would-be attacker must know that we will hit back hard and swiftly. That means heavy emphasis on tactics and strategy geared to repulsing an enemy." The quote was toned down and made more nebulous.

6. Shintaro Ishihara, *The Japan That Can Say No*, 1990, Unauthorized translation. In the official version, page 55, this passage reads, "...this security arrangement is counterproductive. We will protect ourselves with our own strength and wisdom."

7. Ibid.

8. *The New York Times*, October 28, 1990, Op-Ed page.

9. Karel van Wolferen, *The Enigma of Japanese Power*, Vintage Books, 1989 & 1990, p. 42.

10. *Time*, October 29, 1990, p. 54.

11. *Jane's Fighting Ships*, Ninety-fourth edition, 1991-1992, p. 320.

12. *The New York Times*, May 20, 1990, p. A1.

13. *The Wall Street Journal*, April 16, 1990, p. A4.

14. Ibid.

15. Shintaro Ishihara, *The Japan That Can Say No*, 1990, Unauthorized translation. This subject is not covered in the same detail in the official translation.

16. Ibid.

17. Ibid.

18. Ibid.

19. *The Wall Street Journal*, July 5, 1990, "U.S., Korea Appear Near Accord," p. A1.

20. *The Wall Street Journal*, May 11, 1990, "New Arena for Japanese Business: Space," p. D1.

CHAPTER TWELVE

1. *The Wall Street Journal*, February 23, 1990, "Familiar Faces," p. A1.

2. Ibid.

3. Shintaro Ishihara, *The Japan That Can Say No*, 1990, Unauthorized translation. In the official translation, this part of the conversation is deleted.

4. Ibid. In the official translation, 1991, page 94, Ishihara's comment is toned down to, "I asked what trade issues Washington was going to take up next."

5. Telephone interview on March 5, 1992. The Japanese ship their parts to Malaysia or Singapore for assembly there. Consequently, those countries get credit for the export to the U.S., even though it is a Japanese company doing the exporting.

6. *The Wall Street Journal*, February 23, 1990, "Familiar Faces," p. A1.

7. *The New York Times*, September 13, 1990, "Japan's One-Way Lobbying," Editorial page.

8. *The New York Times*, September 16, 1990, "Alain Gomez has Cast...," p. K1.

9. *The Philadelphia Inquirer*, September 16, 1990, "Made in Dixie...," p. C1.

10. Private letter, September 24, 1990.

11. *The Philadelphia Inquirer*, September 16, 1990, "Made in Dixie...," p. C1.

12. *Agents of Influence*, Knopf, Patrick Choate.

CHAPTER THIRTEEN

1. *The New York Times*, Forum Page, July 22, 1990, "Japan Isn't Playing by Different Rules."

2. *International Economic Insights*, January/February 1991, "Rx for America: Export-Led Growth," by C. Fred Bergsten, p. 5.

CHAPTER FOURTEEN

1. Neil Postman, *Amusing Ourselves to Death*, Penguin Books, 1985, p. vii.

Bachmann, Stephen, ed.
Preach Liberty: Selections from the Bible for Progressives
pb: $10.95

Beuys, Joseph.
Energy Plan for the Western Man: Joseph Beuys in America
cl: $18.95

David, Kati.
A Child's War: WW II Through the Eyes of Children
cl: $17.95

Dubuffet, Jean.
Asphyxiating Culture and Other Writings
cl: $17.95

Fried, Ronald K.
Corner Men: Great Boxing Trainers
cl: $21.95

Gould, Jay M., and Goldman, Benjamin.
Deadly Deceit: Low-Level Radiation, High-Level Cover-up
cl:$19.95, pb: $10.95

Hoffman, Abbie.
The Best of Abbie Hoffman: Selections from "Revolution for the Hell of It," "Woodstock Nation", "Steal This Book" and New Writings
cl: $21.95, pb: $14.95

Howard-Howard, Margo (with Abbe Michaels).
I Was a White Slave in Harlem
2nd ed.pb: $12.95

Johnson, Phyllis, and Martin, David, eds.
Frontline Southern Africa: Destructive Engagement
cl: $23.95, pb: $14.95

Jones, E.P.
Where Is Home? Living Through Foster Care
cl: $17.95, pb: $9.95

Null, Gary.
The Complete Guide to Sensible Eating
pb:$14.95
Healing Your Body Naturally: When Traditional Medicine Fails...
pb: $16.95

Null, Gary, and Robins, Howard, D.P.M.
How to Keep Your Feet and Legs Healthy for a Lifetime: The Complete Guide to Foot and Leg Care
pb: $12.95

Ridgeway, James and Casella, Jean.
Cast a Cold Eye: The Best in American Opinion Writing 1990-1991
cl: $24.95, pb: $12.95

Ridgeway, James.
The March to War
pb: $9.95

Taylor, John A.
Notes on an Unhurried Journey
cl: $17.95

Wasserman, Harvey.
Harvey Wasserman's History of the United States
pb: $8.95

Zerden, Sheldon.
The Best of Health
cl: $28.95, pb: $14.95

non-fiction

Four Walls Eight Windows

To order directly from the publisher, please complete the order form below and send with check or money order to: **Four Walls Eight Windows**, PO Box 548, Village Station, New York, NY 10014. For credit card orders only, call 1-800-444-2524 (ext.48) or fax (813) 753-9398.

Qty.	Title	Price

Name _____

Address (no PO Boxes) _____

City/State/Zip _____

Subtotal	
Postage	$2.50
TOTAL	

Prices valid through 12/31/92.

☐ Send me a free catalogue